OUTLAW TALES
of Arizona

True Stories of the Grand Canyon State's Most
Infamous Crooks, Culprits, and Cutthroats

Second Edition

Jan Cleere

TWODOT®

GUILFORD, CONNECTICUT
HELENA, MONTANA
AN IMPRINT OF GLOBE PEQUOT PRESS

To my husband Bob, one of the good guys

To buy books in quantity for corporate use
or incentives, call **(800) 962-0973**
or e-mail **premiums@GlobePequot.com**.

A · TWODOT® · BOOK

TwoDot is an imprint of Globe Pequot Press and a registered trademark of Morris Book Publishing, LLC.

Map © Morris Book Publishing, LLC
Project editor: Meredith Dias
Layout: Lisa Reneson

Library of Congress Cataloging-in-Publication Data is available on file.

ISBN 978-0-7627-7233-9

Printed in the United States of America

10 9 8 7 6 5 4 3 2 1

Contents

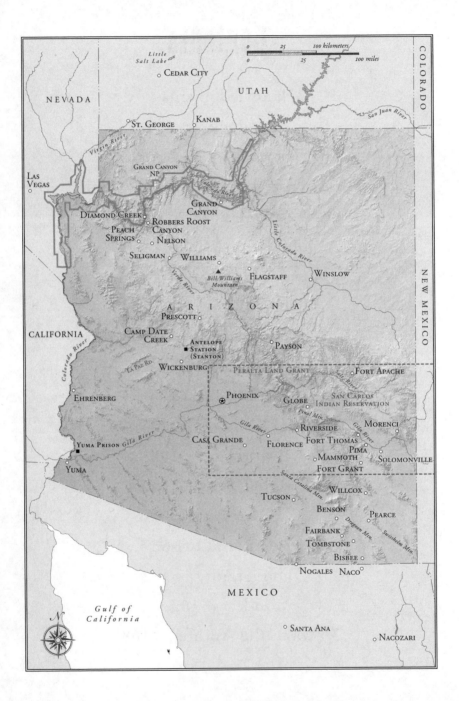

COLORADO

NEVADA

UTAH

Little
Salt Lake

○ CEDAR CITY

○ St. GEORGE ○ KANAB

San Juan River

Virgin River

LAS
VEGAS
○

GRAND CANYON
NP

Colorado River

DIAMOND CREEK
●

GRAND ○
CANYON

PEACH
SPRINGS
○

ROBBERS ROOST
CANYON ●

○ NELSON

Little Colorado River

SELIGMAN ○ ○ WILLIAMS

Verde River

Bill Williams
Mountain ▲ ○ FLAGSTAFF ○ WINSLOW

A   R   I   Z   O   N   A

NEW MEXICO

CALIFORNIA

PRESCOTT ○

CAMP DATE
CREEK ○

ANTELOPE
STATION
(STANTON) ■

La Paz Rd.

○ WICKENBURG

○ PAYSON

PERALTA LAND GRANT

Salt River

○ FORT APACHE

Colorado River

EHRENBERG
○

⊛ PHOENIX

GLOBE ○ SAN CARLOS
INDIAN RESERVATION

Pinal Mtn.

Gila River

○ RIVERSIDE ○ MORENCI

Gila River

YUMA PRISON ■ *Gila River*

CASA GRANDE ○ ○ FLORENCE FORT THOMAS ○

PIMA ○
MAMMOTH ○ ○ SOLOMONVILLE

○ YUMA

FORT GRANT ○

Santa Catalina Mtn. ○ WILLCOX

TUCSON ○ BENSON ○

Dragoon Mtn. ○ PEARCE

Swisshelm Mtn.

FAIRBANK ○
TOMBSTONE ○

BISBEE ○

NOGALES ○ NACO ○

MEXICO

Gulf of
California

○ SANTA ANA

○ NACOZARI

N

0   25   100 kilometers
0   25   100 miles

Acknowledgments

I was fortunate to have the assistance and guidance of the follow-ing individuals, organizations, and institutions while researching *Outlaw Tales of Arizona*. We all share a love of history and a desire to bring the stories of Arizona's past to future generations.

Arizona is graced with a profusion of historians and writers who willingly volunteer their knowledge and expertise. Tucson historian Jim Turner never fails to answer my often obscure questions. His knowledge of Arizona history is truly amazing. Thanks to Mesa Community College historian and instructor Paul T. Hietter; Arizona State Library, Archives and Public Records archivist Nancy Sawyer; and authors Phyllis de la Garza and Wynne Brown for their learned assistance.

I am grateful to the library and research staffs at the Arizona His-torical Society in Tucson, the Special Collections Divisions of the University of Arizona in Tucson and Northern Arizona University in Flagstaff, and the research staff at the Sharlot Hall Museum in Prescott. Their collections are invaluable to any researcher.

Smaller historical societies across Arizona contain fascinat-ing, sometimes unexplored, accounts of our more notorious citizens. I am indebted to H. Christine Reid at the Pinal County Historical Society Museum in Florence, Lynn and Bill Haak at the Gila County Historical Museum in Globe, Ann Garling-house at the Gila County Courthouse, and Ann-Mary J. Lusik, director of the Old Trails Museum in Winslow.

My editors Stephanie Hester and Erin Turner have been staunch supporters of my work, and deserve special recogni-tion for their expertise, guidance, and kind-hearted spirits.

To my family and friends, thanks for keeping me sane when one of these dang desperadoes frustrated me to the brink and I considered hanging every one of them all over again.

Introduction

Uncovering the true history of an outlaw is like trying to tame a rattlesnake. Just when you think you have mastered the complete story of one of these desperadoes, some new piece of evidence surfaces that poisons your theories to the bone.

Contradictions abound for those researching the lives and legends of elusive lawbreakers. It is these unsolved mysteries that keep historians and writers sequestered in dusty, spider-webbed archives thumbing with ink-stained fingers through crumbling newspapers and ancient parchments, searching for that elusive, as yet undiscovered document that will make their work more true and compelling than all previously written. Sometimes, I suspect these long-ago outlaws are sitting around their campfires in hell laughing at those of us trying to make sense of the legacies they left behind.

Arizona claims its share of these varmints whose lives are complicated by myth, mystique, and a goodly dose of mayhem. In fact the abundance of crooks roaming through Arizona Territory in the rough and often violent 1800s was one of the factors that kept statehood at bay until 1912. Their misdeeds ran the gamut from train and stagecoach robbery, horse and cattle rustling to murder, larceny, and fraud.

Lawmen disagreed about how many of these desperadoes actually called Arizona home. Some claimed only about fifteen really bad guys roamed the territory while others insisted over three hundred came from across the nation looking for gold, silver, copper, and unsuspecting, naive individuals to rob, swindle, and slay.

Outlaws were so prevalent in Arizona Territory that in 1877 Governor Anson Peacely-Killen Safford ranted that they "are a scourge to civilization, a disgrace to humanity, and should be swept from the face of the earth as remorsely as the most ferocious wild beast." Five years later, the *Tombstone Epitaph*, still searching for a way to rid Arizona, and particularly the town of Tombstone, of its criminal element suggested "[making] it incumbent upon, not only officials, but all good citizens as well, to take such positive measures as will speedily rid this section of that murderous, thieving element which has made us a reproach before the world, and so seriously retarded the industry and progress of our country."

While Governor Safford was still in office (1869–1877), construction began in 1875 on Yuma Territorial Prison to house Arizona's numerous lawbreakers. More than three thousand prisoners, including twenty-nine women, were incarcerated in the adobe and stone structure until it was replaced in 1909 by a new prison in Florence. Only twenty-six managed to escape from Yuma, although many more tried.

But even while these miscreants were serving time or swinging from the end of a rope or dying from a dozen bullets plugged through their evil hearts, we were intrigued by their stories and devoured every word we heard and read. At times one story contradicted another, but we continued to amass these tales and often passed them along as truths. We relished hearing about the lawman gone bad and the outlaw with the heart of gold.

Today we continue to search for a substantiated fact or an ancient document that will prove the yarn told to us by a crusty old miner or sun-crazed cowboy. And maybe we will eventually unearth more facts about these outlaw men and women and toss aside the legends and mythology that have kept us spellbound for more than one hundred years. But sometimes I wonder if we will enjoy the truth as much as the fiction. Mystery and history go hand in hand, and Arizona history contains some of the best whodunits around.

The murderers and scoundrels presented in these pages come from all across the inhospitable wilderness territory, perpetrating their crimes on innocent pioneers attempting to settle an unforgiving land. Not everything about them can be proved beyond a reasonable doubt, leaving the reader's imagination to decide how much to believe and what should remain as just a good tale.

The Wickenburg Massacre
Last Ride Out of Town

Just after sunup on November 5, 1871, the Arizona Stage Company coach, crowded with eight passengers, pulled out of Wickenburg for its run to the Colorado River town of Ehrenberg , a distance of just over one hundred miles. All but one individual had started the journey the evening before in Prescott. Aaron Barnett first boarded in Wickenburg and settled in beside his sleepy riding companions. Just a few miles outside of Wickenburg, he realized he had forgotten some unfinished business in town. Asking the driver to stop, Barnett got off and watched as the carriage again headed west toward Ehrenberg before he set out on foot the few short miles back to Wickenburg. Whatever Barnett forgot to do that day saved his life. Of the remaining seven passengers and one driver on the ill-fated stage, six would never live to see the sun rise again.

"Dutch" John Lance had been employed by the Arizona Stage Company just a few weeks when he took the reins of the four-horse coach early that Monday morning. This would be only his second trip down the well-traveled La Paz Road from Wickenburg to Ehrenberg. There were always reports of Indians waylaying travelers and even some instances of murder along the central Arizona route, but he had no intention of letting his passengers fall to such a fate before he deposited them in Ehrenberg. From there most would take a steamer for the run downriver to Yuma and on to California. As he inspected the wagon one last time, he watched his travelers climb on board.

They had enjoyed but a few hours rest after arriving from Prescott well after midnight.

Peter Hamel and George Salmon climbed inside the coach, glad to be returning to their families in California after working with the Wheeler expedition, one of four research missions exploring western territories. The results brought back by these parties would include topographic and geologic maps, inventory of flora, fauna, strata, and mineral resources, plus interpretations of geologic occurrences. George M. Wheeler's survey was the only military expedition and had concentrated on water and terrain, studies that would affect future military operations.

Twenty-two-year-old journalist Frederick Wadsworth Loring had also traveled with the Wheeler expedition, reporting back to eastern publications. Before he left on the tour, Loring trimmed his hair very short and jokingly remarked that the Apaches would not find him a worthy adversary with so few locks to scalp. He chose to ride next to the driver.

Climbing up beside Loring and Lance, Charles S. Adams, who had been working in the flour depot of W. Bichard & Co. in Prescott, was grateful to be heading home to his wife and children in San Francisco.

Frederick Shoholm settled inside the coach beside Hamel and Salmon. Shoholm had recently sold his jewelry business in Prescott and was on his way to Philadelphia. He planned to board a ship in San Francisco and travel by way of Panama.

The only woman on the stage, twenty-four-year-old Mollie Sheppard, also had sold her business in Prescott and was reportedly carrying as much as $15,000 in cash, plus a large stash of jewelry. Mollie had run a successful house of pleasure

Monument dedicated to the victims of the Wickenburg Massacre
Arizona State Library, Archives and Public Records, History and Archives Division, Phoenix
#95-9803

since 1868, but it was time to get out of town and start else-where. She planned on settling in Panama City.

William Kruger, a clerk with Arizona Territory's Army Quartermaster, would leave the stage in Ehrenberg where he had business to conduct. Supposedly he was carrying between $30,000 and $40,000 in military funds. Kruger's blemished reputation included a suspicion that he sometimes made a tidy profit from the sale of army mules and equipment.

Once Aaron Barnett left the stage to walk back to Wickenburg, the remaining passengers started a card game of Freeze-Out, a popular gambling pastime. Mollie graciously spread her luxurious fur cape across everyone's knees to serve as a table. As was often the case, most of the passengers placed their weapons under the seat cushions so they could enjoy a more comfortable ride.

The stagecoach clipped along for the next hour without a hitch. About eight miles out of Wickenburg, Dutch Lance had just started the horses into a wash when he saw the spindly bushes beside the road come to life. "Apaches!" he shouted as a band of marauders quickly surrounded the carriage, firearms blazing a torrent of bullets. The first salvo hit Lance dead on. As he dropped the reins, the horses careened off the road.

Inside the coach, Shoholm died with cards still in his hand, and Hamel fell across Mollie's fur coat. Within seconds another round of gunfire ratcheted across the wagon. Bullets slammed into Adams's spine, leaving him paralyzed and at the mercy of his assailants. Loring fell with a knife imbedded in his chest. Although Salmon managed to flee the coach, he was brought down within minutes.

Kruger, suffering only minor wounds, later claimed he threw the hysterical and wounded Mollie to the floor of the wagon to protect her from further gunfire. When the shooting abruptly ceased after just two volleys and a deadly calm enveloped the bloody wagon, Kruger waited only seconds before shoving Mollie out of the stage into the desert.

According to Kruger's later testimony, several gunmen chased the fleeing couple, but he managed to fight them off, even wounding two with his deadly aim, all the while keeping the fainting Mollie tucked under his arm. However, one report credits Mollie with doing her share by threatening the approaching desperadoes with a broken whiskey bottle.

Kruger claimed the assailants pursued the two a short distance before scattering across the desert like a herd of cattle on the run.

The couple struggled along the desolate road until they spotted a mail wagon coming their way. The driver was horrified at the tale he heard and seeing Mollie's festering injuries—three bullet wounds plus wooden splinters from the coach deeply embedded in her arm—he sequestered the pair behind his wagon, gave them an ample supply of water, and rode off on a spare horse toward Wickenburg to report the ghastly killings. Kruger and Mollie were taken to Camp Date Creek for medical treatment with Mollie still clinging to her precious fur cape, its plush elegance riddled with nine bullet holes.

The dead were returned to Wickenburg for burial. Only Salmon was buried at the site and his body was eventually exhumed and interred beside the others. When the *Arizona Miner* reported the incident, it noted Salmon ". . . received a severe wound and fell from the stage, but recovering ran about twenty yards, was followed, overtaken, killed and scalped, the whole hair, ears, skin of the face being taken off to the mouth."

"Six men," said the *Miner*, "who . . . left Wickenburg full of life and hope and in the happy anticipation of soon again greeting their friends after a prolonged absence—lay side by side, rigid in death and drenched in blood—the unavenged victims of a murder as dark and as damnable as ever stained the hands of an assassin."

Kruger and Mollie survived their injuries and eventually made it to California. A few years later, Kruger reported that Mollie had succumbed to her wounds. She never made it to Panama City.

As the sole survivor, William Kruger often related his version of the Wickenburg Massacre, and many believed every word he said. Others, to this day, question several of his details of the slaying. There are almost as many opinions of who attacked the Wickenburg stagecoach that crisp November morning as there were victims of the massacre and mayhem.

Initial reaction placed blame on the Apache-Mohave (Yavapai) Indians sequestered at Camp Date Creek, about twenty-five miles from Wickenburg. Ironically, the camp was established to protect travelers along the La Paz Road. The attacking warriors, who were horseless, purportedly wore moccasins specific to the Apache-Mohave. The tribe formed its moccasins by pulling the upper part of its leather footgear down over the lower section and lacing it to the sole with rawhide, creating a distinct foot pattern. Other tribes in the area pulled the leather up around the top of the foot, leaving a smoother footprint.

The posse followed a trail that led to Camp Date Creek. Along the way they discovered a hunting bag containing bone powder, a sacred medicine among the Apache-Mohave. They also found a deck of cards with the corners cut off, a practice of local Natives. One of the most bizarre pieces of evidence investigated was excrement found at the massacre site that supposedly contained mesquite beans, a favorite of Indians in the area. Upon further investigation, the beans were found to be pumpkin seeds, which local tribes rarely ate.

Within days of the massacre, several Apache-Mohave showed up with cash in their pockets and were immediately suspected of participating in the massacre. But the Wells Fargo box left at the murder scene, purportedly containing a great deal of cash, had not been opened.

Two men were scalped—Salmon and Hamel—and this almost solidified the argument that Indians had instigated the Wickenburg Massacre.

Other evidence surfaced that led some to question whether Indians perpetrated the attack. Indians would not have left surviving horses (the lead horse had been killed and another wounded), as horsemeat was a favorite dish. Colorful shawls, jewelry, and even the horses' leather harness would have been confiscated if Indians had been the culprits since these were highly valued items. The surviving horses had been freed and the harness found neatly stacked. Indians would not have wasted time on this task.

Some of the mailbags were cut open, but the envelopes found strewn across the desert had been carefully torn off at one end, not ripped apart. Ammunition was left at the scene. Indians desperately needed ammunition and would not have ignored this stash.

The posse found no other tracks along the path traveled by William Kruger and Mollie Sheppard. If Indians had followed them, the couple would not have escaped—warring Indians rarely left survivors.

Kruger and Mollie both claimed they saw about fifteen men clad in blue soldier's trousers, standard issue for reservation Indians, coming at them with pistols blazing, but neither could positively say whether they were Indians, Mexicans, or white men.

Another faction held local Anglos guilty of purposely pointing the finger of blame at the Indians. Businessmen made money when native tribes rebelled as this forced the federal government to pump more money and troops into the territory.

Yet another conjecture blamed Mexican bandits for the attack, led by the nefarious outlaw Joaquin Barbe. About two months before the massacre, a Mexican woman living in Wickenburg claimed she overheard a conversation between two Mexican men plotting a stage robbery. She warned her friends not to take the Wickenburg stage for the next few months.

In 1916 a dying man said he still carried a silver watch fob bearing the letter "L" that he had obtained from a Mexican woman in Wickenburg about three months after the robbery. He claimed the watch fob belonged to the reporter Frank Loring.

Mollie Sheppard believed a group of Anglo men from Prescott, who had shown a keen interest in how much money she was carrying, might be responsible for the slaughter.

Since only the bags of Mollie and Kruger were broken into, a small group even suspected the couple may have perpetrated the biggest hoax by killing the passengers, burying all the money they could carry into the desert, inflicting wounds upon themselves, and walking away from the ordeal much richer. Kruger claimed the attackers got away with close to $25,000.

Inspection of Kruger's gun when he arrived at Camp Date Creek showed it had not been fired even though he swore he had shot two of the attackers.

Debate still lingers over who laid in ambush for the Wickenburg stage as it bounced along the La Paz Road that cool November morning. Did the perpetrators kill for money, for revenge, or maybe just for sport? We may never know.

Journalist Fred Loring wrote of his experiences with the Wheeler expedition shortly before boarding the Wickenburg stage that fateful day. "I am bootless, coatless, everything but lifeless," he said. "I have had a fortnight of horrors. This morning an Indian fight capped the climax. However, I am well and cheerful." He had no idea what was in store for him.

Frank Nashville
"Buckskin Frank" Leslie
The Lady Killer

May Leslie's knees buckled as she awaited the next volley of gunfire. The slightest movement from her might be her last, and she commanded her body to remain as rigid as a rotting corpse as bullets whizzed about her head. Maybe one more round would satisfy the gunman. She heard the bullets click into the chamber as her husband prepared to fire again. He always took careful aim, as careful as anyone full of liquor could muster.

May watched him sway as he pointed the gun at her head. He slowly pulled the trigger and painted her portrait in bullets along the wall. As the gun clattered to the ground, so did Frank Leslie in a drunken stupor. May, known around Tombstone, Arizona, as the "Silhouette Girl" because of her husband's proclivity for shooting around her profile, fell in a trembling heap. She had survived seven years of marriage to Frank Leslie, a man of sweet charm and deadly aim, but she figured her odds of surviving one more year were not good.

Frank Leslie had been hanging around Tombstone since 1880, earning a reputation as a hard-drinking, free-fisted, fast-shooting, story-telling lady's man. He related so many versions of his origins that even he probably did not remember the truth. He usually claimed he was born in the early 1840s in Texas, but once told a reporter his family roots were in Virginia. He also said he served in the Confederate Army as a bugler; studied medicine in Heidelberg, Germany; served as a deputy sheriff in Kansas under Wild Bill Hickok; prospected in Colorado; been a roughrider in Australia and a boat pilot in the Fiji Islands; owned a bar in San Francisco; and ridden as an army scout in the Dakotas, Oklahoma, Texas, and along Arizona's borders. Somewhere he acquired the nickname "Buckskin Frank" and dressed to suit the title in a fringed buckskin jacket.

Of course Leslie never offered any proof of his past whereabouts or his accomplishments. Texas and Virginia birth records do not exist for Frank Nashville Leslie. Neither are there records of him serving in the Confederate Army, of him attending a Heidelberg medical school, or of any lawman named Leslie riding with Hickok.

However, a couple of his stories have a semblance of truth. He probably did serve as a scout on the San Carlos Indian Reservation around 1877. And he tended bar in a couple of saloons in San Francisco until moseying into Tombstone.

Tombstone in 1880 was a town filled with gambling dens, saloons, and houses of pleasure. Leslie found work bartending at the Cosmopolitan Hotel, a two-story wooden building boasting a veranda, ladies' parlor, and sitting rooms. The saloon advertised a variety of wines, liquors, "and the finest brands of cigars." When not working behind the bar, Leslie could be found visiting any number of Tombstone saloons imbibing enough liquor to satisfy an entire herd of trail-dry cattle. His proclivity for whiskey was only surpassed by his eye for the ladies, and he dressed to please them in his buckskin jacket, custom-made boots, and pearl-studded shirts.

May Killeen had recently separated from her husband, Mike, and taken a room at the Cosmopolitan. She and Leslie had already exchanged pleasantries on more than one occasion. On the night of June 22, 1880, May asked Leslie to escort her home from a dance, and Leslie was more than happy to oblige. They headed for the hotel accompanied by Leslie's friend, George Perine. No one noticed the shadowy figure watching as they entered the hotel.

Now Mike Killeen had already warned Leslie to stay away from his wife, and Leslie had taken the precaution of borrowing a gun for the evening. It was against the law to carry weapons in Tombstone; firearms must be surrendered at the first saloon encountered upon entering town. But those who felt the need of protection could always borrow a gun from behind the bar. Leslie had no problem obtaining a weapon for his evening stroll with May Killeen.

Mike Killeen watched the threesome enter the hotel and wasted no time following his wayward wife and Frank Leslie. George Perine headed for the bar while Leslie and May made their way to the second-floor veranda. From his place at the bar, Perine saw Killeen enter the hotel. He shouted to Leslie that Killeen was on his way with murder in his eye and a gun in his hand.

The roar of gunfire sent hotel guests stumbling sleepily from their rooms only to hastily retreat behind locked doors as the two men emptied their guns. Killeen tumbled down the stairs and into the saloon with Leslie in hot pursuit. From behind the bar, Leslie grabbed a second pistol and fired another round at Killeen. When the smoke cleared, Killeen lay mortally wounded. He lingered for six days, long enough to swear Leslie started the ruckus. Leslie insisted Killeen came in shooting and he had no recourse but to return fire.

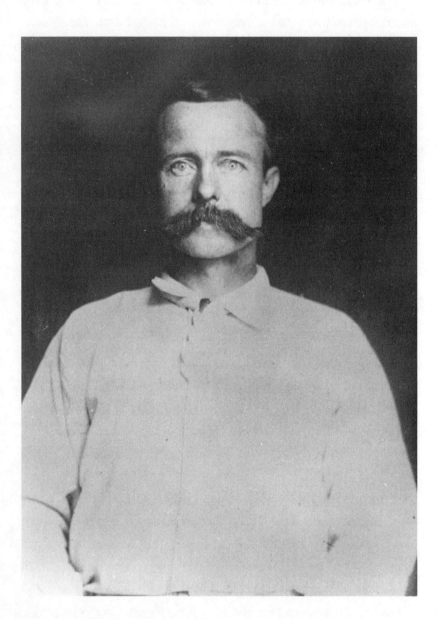

Frank Nashville "Buckskin Frank" Leslie, photo circa 1893
Arizona State Library, Archives and Public Records, History and Archives Division,
Phoenix #97-7081

Arrested and charged with Mike Killeen's murder, Leslie relied on his own testimony and that of the not-so-grieving widow to swear Killeen came onto the veranda with gun blazing. It did not take the coroner's jury long to acquit Leslie on the grounds of self-defense.

On August 5, just weeks after Leslie was released from jail, the same judge who officiated at Leslie's court hearing pronounced Frank Leslie and May Killeen man and wife. The ceremony took place in the parlor of the Cosmopolitan Hotel. The *Tombstone Epitaph* congratulated the couple on their nuptials, lauding Leslie as *"un chavalier sans peur et sans reproche"* (a knight without fear and reproach).

Leslie eventually moved down the street to the Oriental Saloon to work for owner Milt Joyce. The Earp brothers hung out at the Oriental and Leslie was welcome to drink with them, but he took no part in the infamous October 26, 1881, shootout at the O. K. Corral. Wyatt always said Leslie had the second fastest draw in the territory, just behind Doc Holliday.

Over the years Leslie developed an interest in prospecting and filed several mining claims in the nearby Dragoon and Swisshelm Mountains. But he preferred life in town where drinking, gambling, and a little "bird" watching embodied his nightly pleasures. When he had money, he spent it. When he did not get what he wanted, he turned surly and dangerous. May Leslie soon learned to dread those nights. As old-time Tombstone resident Billy King once said, Leslie "was a likable damn fellow when he was sober . . . but when he was tanked up he turned as sour as a barrel of Dago red."

Leslie's quick draw earned him a reputation on both sides of the badge. In March 1881, a detachment of eight lawmen set out from Tombstone on the trail of bandits who had held up the stagecoach as it headed toward Benson. The posse consisted of Wyatt, Virgil, and Morgan Earp; Cochise County Sheriff Johnny Behan and Deputy Sheriff Billy Breakenridge; and sworn-in deputies Doc Holliday, Bat Masterson, and Frank Leslie. Separating as they traveled, Leslie came upon one of the outlaws and reportedly sat down to eat with him before returning alone to Tombstone claiming he had lost the trail. Rumors circulated that Sheriff Behan, supposedly a friend of the robbers, had paid Leslie to ride a cold course.

The sun had barely risen above the horizon when Leslie walked into the Oriental Saloon on November 14, 1882, but already a group of men hovered near the bar having their usual liquored breakfast. Leslie was welcomed into their discussion, which may have had political overtones, and the men finished several rounds before cocky young Billy Claiborne entered the saloon about 7:30 a.m. Claiborne was as mean as an angry snake. He had ridden with the murdering cattle rustler John Ringo and often worked both sides of the border stealing cattle and horses. Claiborne blamed Leslie for Ringo's untimely demise just a few months prior—Leslie and Ringo had been seen together shortly before Ringo was found straddling a tree with a bullet in his head.

It was obvious Claiborne had downed his breakfast at a neighboring watering hole. He sidled up to the group at the bar and immediately interrupted the conversation. Leslie took him aside and asked him to leave. Claiborne refused and again butted into the assemblage. Leslie booted Claiborne out the saloon door. Claiborne shouted he would return to get even, but Leslie just turned his back on the youngster.

When Claiborne reappeared, he was carrying his Winchester rifle. The street emptied as he headed toward the Oriental. "I don't allow any man to spit on me," he swore.

Leslie, warned that Claiborne was looking for him, left the saloon by a side door. Rounding the corner to the main street, he saw Claiborne hiding behind a fruit stand and warned the youngster not to shoot. But Claiborne stood up and fired, the bullet landing harmlessly at Leslie's feet. Leslie floored him with one shot. "I told him I was sorry," Leslie later stated. "I might have done more, but I couldn't do less."

Again facing a coroner's jury and pleading self-defense, Leslie walked out of the courtroom a free man.

Milt Joyce, proprietor of the Oriental Saloon, also owned the Magnolia Ranch in the Swisshelm Mountains east of Tombstone. Leslie had a one-quarter interest in the place and Joyce left most of the ranching business in Leslie's hands. Since Leslie spent more time there than Joyce, the Magnolia was often mistakenly called Leslie's ranch.

In 1883 Leslie experienced a run-in with Apache raiders at the Magnolia. He lost most of the horses and about fifty head of cattle to the marauders. Two years later, in May 1885, when Geronimo and a band of Apaches escaped from the San Carlos Indian Reservation, Leslie was more than happy to hire on as a scout under Captain Wirt Davis to hunt down the notorious Apache warrior. It took three months of hard riding before Davis and his men located Geronimo's camp. And although Geronimo escaped, the soldiers killed a handful of his men and captured a few women and children.

Davis sent Leslie to inform General George Crook of the battle. According to Leslie, he had to swim the Bavispe River eleven times in one day to deliver the report. Leslie knew how to make himself look good in the eyes of the law.

Each time Leslie returned from scouting, battling Apaches, and even one stint as an inspector along the Arizona-Sonora border looking for smugglers, he made up for lost time in the Tombstone saloons. He would then go home to May, slap her around, and stand her up against the wall to practice his shooting. May knew she would soon perish beneath his hands or at the end of his gun. On May 27, 1887, she filed for divorce, claiming Leslie beat and choked her along with framing her silhouette in bullets. She also accused him of infidelity. The court awarded May half of Leslie's interest in the Magnolia Ranch, which she immediately sold back to Milt Joyce. Leslie eventually sold Joyce his remaining interest, but continued to manage the place.

He was soon seen dallying with Mollie Williams, also known as Mollie Bradshaw, Mollie Edwards, and Blonde Mollie, a singer at the Bird Cage Theater. She had arrived in town with a man named Mike Bradshaw. Shortly after Leslie made Mollie's acquaintance, Bradshaw lay dead with his head bashed in. Fingers pointed at Leslie, but no evidence was found implicating him. He and Mollie headed off into the Swisshelms and the Magnolia Ranch.

Unfortunately they did not stay put on the ranch and often spent days frequenting drinking establishments from one end of Tombstone to the other. Mollie could hold her own with Leslie and the two often loudly disagreed well into the night as they guzzled copious amounts of liquor.

In early July 1889, the couple headed into Tombstone to celebrate Independence Day. Their revelry continued for almost a week. Finally, hitching up their horses, they headed out of town, drunk when they left and still sotted when they arrived back at the ranch on July 10. An argument started in Tombstone continued to rage.

The next day, Leslie, still swilling a potent brew, rode over to William Reynolds's ranch to inform his neighbor he was going to kill him. He ordered Reynolds to defend himself, but when Reynolds, who had obviously seen Leslie in this condition before, refused to pick up a rifle, Leslie left in a huff and staggered home.

James Neal worked off and on for Leslie at the Magnolia Ranch. He understood his boss's frequent fits of rage and usually stayed out of sight when trouble boiled. But on the night of July 11, he took pity on the tipsy Mollie and sat with her while Leslie was off harassing his neighbor. When Leslie returned, he suspected Neal and Mollie had been up to no good. After smacking Mollie around a few times, he determined he would "put a stop to all this." He picked up his pistol and aimed. With one shot, Mollie fell dead to the floor in a heap of skirts and petticoats.

Neal had no time to react before Leslie fired at him. "Don't be afraid, it's nothing," Leslie told him and, at first, Neal believed him. But as blood started trailing down his legs, Neal bolted through the door and into the desert. The next day, rancher Reynolds found him collapsed on his doorstep.

Leslie came looking for Neal at the Reynolds ranch and related the evening's events, claiming Neal had killed Mollie and he had shot Neal in self-defense. Reynolds denied seeing Neal, so Leslie assumed the young man lay dead somewhere in the desert and figured there would be no witnesses to dispute his story.

After Leslie left, Reynolds sent for the doctor who patched up Neal and took him into town. Neal told his story to the sheriff leaving little doubt who had perpetrated the double shooting.

Two days later, deputies found a disheveled Leslie riding along the road and took him to the sheriff. Proclaiming his distress and grief over losing his beloved Mollie, Leslie confessed to killing Neal after Neal had slain Mollie. Suddenly, Neal appeared in the doorway, weak but strong enough to call Leslie a liar.

This time the jury did not agree with Leslie's self-defense argument and sentenced him to serve the remainder of his life in the Yuma Territorial Prison for the murder of Blonde Mollie.

Leslie and ten other prisoners were escorted from the Cochise County Jail to Yuma Prison in January 1890 under the watchful eye of Sheriff John Slaughter. According to the *Tucson Citizen*, they all arrived drunk. Maybe Leslie was able to persuade the sheriff to make one last stop before sending him into the depths of hell.

Leslie actually spent only seven years in Yuma Prison. There was talk he was part of an attempted breakout in March 1890, but no mention of the incident appears in prison records. For the most part, he was a model prisoner and spent most of his time working in the prison infirmary as a pharmacist.

In 1893 a reporter from the *San Francisco Chronicle* visited Leslie at the prison. He must have believed every word out of Leslie's mouth as the story he wrote comprises tall tales right from Leslie's vivid imagination. When Belle Stowell of San Francisco read the *Chronicle* article, she began corresponding with Leslie and sending gifts of food and clothing to the imprisoned man. Eventually their friendship blossomed into love.

Leslie's exemplary behavior behind bars, along with the pleas of Belle Stowell and other friends who petitioned Arizona Territorial Governor Benjamin Franklin for his release, set him free on November 17, 1896. He ran right into the arms of the waiting Belle and the two were married in Stockton, California, on December 1.

How long the marriage lasted is uncertain for Belle soon disappeared from Leslie's life. He went to Mexico in early 1897 to assist a geologist seeking coal deposits for the Southern Pacific Railroad. While there, he supposedly killed three men attempting to steal wood from the work site.

Leslie may have headed next for the Alaskan goldfields, but by 1902, he was back in San Francisco. When the *Chronicle* reported he sustained a gunshot wound after his pistol fell out of his pocket and went off, he told the reporter, "I suppose that my friends will tell me I'm not fit to carry a pistol. After forty years on the frontier to be hurt by my own gun, looks like it."

Leslie worked as a stocker for a couple of grocery stores and as a janitor in a billiard hall, but he usually lived off handouts from the barrooms he frequented. Wyatt Earp, now living in California, sometimes staked his old friend to a set of clean clothes and maybe a drink or two.

Leslie was last seen alive around 1920, sweeping floors in a San Francisco saloon. One night he disappeared, supposedly taking the bartender's gun with him. Maybe he was just borrowing it like he used to do in Tombstone. About three years later, a skeleton and rusty gun were found in the hills north of Martinez, California. The serial number on the gun was the same as the one taken from the bar that night. "If it [the story] is indeed real," said writer/historian Douglas Martin, "then Leslie was not all bad; he did one good thing before he died. He killed himself."

Leslie once admitted to killing thirteen men. "It was my fourteenth that caused all my trouble," he bemoaned. "But then, my fourteenth was a woman."

The Grime/Hawley Heist
A Tale from the Hanging Tree

"I don't want to die with my boots on!" cried Lafayette Grime as he squatted on the dust-encrusted ground and took off a pair of very petite shoes—size four. He gazed above him at the huge sycamore tree that spanned the width of the road. Across one of its broad boughs, two thick ropes swayed in the night's light breeze. One noose would soon encircle the young man's neck. The other was for his partner, Curtis Hawley, who angrily scoffed when the Reverend D. W. Calfee offered to pray with the condemned men. "What the devil is the future to me," Hawley growled. "It's the present that's bothering me. I want to get away from this mob."

More than one hundred men watched as the diminutive Lafayette, barely out of his teens, unsteadily rose from the ground in his stocking feet. He had already fainted once and the crowd waited to see if he would die of fright before the noose did its work. When the order was given, dozens of hands willingly pulled the ropes that sent Lafayette V. Grime and Curtis B. Hawley to their deaths. Only four days prior, on August 20, 1882, they had enjoyed reputations as upstanding citizens in the town of Globe. Now they would forever be known as the most inept robbers and murderers in the young history of Arizona Territory.

Lafayette Grime, his older brother Cicero, and their friend Curtis Hawley were also three of the most unlikely road builders in Arizona. However, their attempt to construct a thoroughfare from the town of Pinal, just south of Globe, to the hamlet of Riverside, about thirty miles away, was the impetus that started them down the path to the ropes dangling from the sycamore tree.

Fair-haired Lafayette "Fate" Grime, a very slight man with unbelievably small feet, made his living tapping around Globe as a dance instructor. He supplemented his income by working in the mines and mills when money got tight on the dance floor. Cicero Grime, a photographer by trade, had recently established a construction company, Grime & Company, which was the operational base for their new venture. Curtis Hawley ran a wood and charcoal business providing materials to local mining companies.

The three men submitted a bid of $1,800 to build the wagon road, and their proposal was accepted on the condition they obtain a bond. Problem was, the road was going to cost about $4,000 to complete.

When they failed to secure a bond in the time allotted, the novice road builders requested and were given an extension until April 1, 1882. When that day came and went with no bond posted, the contract went to the next lowest bidder.

Undaunted, the men planned to build a bridge at the lower end of town. But as they talked through the logistics of such an undertaking, one of them suggested that robbing a stagecoach would be a lot easier and much more rewarding. From this casual remark, the three soon-to-be outlaws inaugurated plans to rob a Wells Fargo shipment as the buckboard coach made its way through the Pinal Mountains from Casa Grande to Globe. These carriages often toted mail and payrolls of gold to local mines.

Not all stages were fully enclosed carriages. An open buckboard wagon was more adept at handling the rough roads through the Pinals. Even then, trails to the mines deep within the mountains often required shipments be transferred to mule teams to maneuver the sometimes treacherous and often inaccessible pathways.

When the men heard a large shipment was coming through on Sunday, August 20, they headed about four miles into the mountains to Pioneer Pass where the road careened around a sharp bend. Lafayette and Curtis hunkered down behind a massive boulder and waited.

The bandits had no intention of shooting anyone, just slowing the mules and scaring away the driver. Along with Curtis's .44-caliber rifle and Lafayette's .50-caliber Springfield, they brought with them a miner's pickax and a hatchet. Fearing their horses would give them away, they left their steeds back in Globe.

Leaving his brother and Curtis behind the rock, Cicero, the spotter, steered his horse down the trail toward the expected payload. His job was to peacefully intercept the buckboard stage and determine if it carried a stash lucrative enough to warrant the holdup.

Muleskinner Frank Porter also waited for the Wells Fargo wagon. As he steadied his six-mule team, he was glad to see Cicero Grime riding his way. Porter would transfer the heavy gold payroll to his mules for the ride up to the mining camp, and he was grateful to have Cicero's help to lighten the workload. As soon as the buckboard, driven by Wells Fargo messenger Andy Hall, came to a halt, the men began hauling the gold off the wagon and onto the mules. Hall had already distinguished himself in Arizona history by serving with Major John Wesley Powell on the first successful trek through the Grand Canyon in 1869.

Curiosity got the better of Cicero as he tied a strongbox to Porter's lead mule. When Hall told him the box contained $5,000 in gold for the Mike Morris Mine, Cicero suppressed a satisfied sneer and quickly tightened the straps an extra notch. Picking up his horse's reins, he bade the two men so long and casually sauntered up the trail toward the hidden gunmen.

Reaching the boulder where Lafayette and Curtis lay in wait, Cicero alerted the men that the Wells Fargo shipment contained a sizeable amount of gold and the heist was on. He warned that Hall, who was leading the pack train, had a gun, but that Porter, bringing up the rear, carried no weapon. Cicero then headed back into Globe to give himself an alibi for the day's upcoming events.

Hall drove the mules cautiously. He knew one unsteady move would spook the creatures and he did not want any missteps until he delivered the hefty payload to the mine. As he approached the towering boulder, flanked by a steep incline on the other side of the trail, he slowed the mules to the pace of a well-fed snail.

Without warning Lafayette and Curtis opened fire, quickly killing the lead mule. Before Hall could react, another barrage of bullets sent him scurrying out of harm's way. He shouted to Porter, who had not yet reached the pass, to hightail it into Globe and bring help—fast.

Hall hastily put greater distance between himself and the gunmen. Too far away to see them clearly, he assumed they were Apaches since several attacks had occurred recently in the vicinity. As he took aim, he saw two men slashing the ropes holding the strongbox to the now dead, treasure-laden mule. His shots missed but return fire found its mark and Hall hobbled away with a bullet through his thigh.

With his hatchet Lafayette hacked open the strongbox, swiftly transferred the money to his saddlebags, then swung the bags over his shoulder, ready to hightail it into the hills. Curtis wanted to sort through the registered mail for other lucrative loot, but Lafayette was already on the move, leaving the burly woodcutter to follow dutifully in the dancer's diminutive footsteps.

Before long, the two bandits came upon Dr. F. W. Vail who was leading a packhorse loaded with supplies to his mine. The well-respected Globe druggist had heard the gunfire and asked the men if they knew what had happened. Lafayette and Curtis offered up that they suspected Indians were in the area and the three of them should press on together toward Globe. Dr. Vail unloaded his packhorse so the two horseless bandits could travel more expeditiously.

About a mile down the road, Lafayette and Curtis got jittery about Vail. They returned his horse and let the pharmacist get a few yards away before Curtis whipped out his gun and cowardly shot him in the back. Lafayette obligingly plugged a couple more bullets into the dying man.

Heading off on both of Vail's horses, the two men next ran into Hall who still believed Apaches had attacked the mule team. Hall showed the bandits the bullet he had extracted from his thigh and urged them to join him in searching for the fugitives. Lafayette and Curtis agreed, but the novice desperadoes soon grew uneasy, particularly when Hall exhibited an increasing interest in Lafayette's overstuffed and very heavy saddlebags. Allowing Hall to get a few feet ahead, they opened fire. With his

Sycamore hanging tree in Globe used to hang Lafayette Grime and Curtis Hawley
Gila County Historical Society, Globe, Arizona, photo GM #36-2

gun still in hand, Hall dropped dead to the ground, his trigger finger erratically sent a burst of gunfire into the air.

Not daring to take Dr. Vail's horses into Globe for fear the mounts would be recognized, the men headed out on foot, stopping only to divide the loot into three equal shares and burying it near Russell Gulch, each keeping a few of the $20 gold pieces for spending money. They then made their way, separately, back to town.

By now muleskinner Porter had arrived in Globe and sounded the alarm. Church bells rang out as a posse, headed by Gila County Sheriff William W. Lowther, took off into the mountains and the robbery site.

Around sundown, they came upon Dr. Vail, not far from death but able to identify his attackers as men he had seen around Globe: "one a big dark guy, the other a small fair-haired younger man."

Not much later the search party stumbled across Hall's body, sporting enough bullet holes to raise hairs on a rattlesnake's hide.

At the robbery site they quickly discovered the bandits' hiding spot and distinguished two sets of footprints behind the boulder, one so small they looked as if they belonged to a woman. From this shred of evidence, plus Dr. Vail's description of his assailants, the sheriff had a good idea who had committed the crimes. Only one man in town wore shoes that petite.

Within hours after the shooting, rewards totaling $6,000 were posted for the capture of the individual or persons responsible for the slayings of Dr. Vail and Andy Hall.

As the bodies of the two slain men were laid to rest on Monday, a mournful Cicero Grime volunteered to toll the bell for the funeral procession. Curtis decided the safest place for him was at home. Lafayette only stuck around long enough to return the rifle he had borrowed before heading for Wheatfields on the pretext of having work to do. Unfortunately, he forgot to clean the gun before returning it. The owner, somewhat suspicious of the condition of his rifle, took it to the gunsmith shop where the cartridges were compared with those found at the murder sites. The match was close enough to alert Sheriff Lowther.

On Tuesday, acting on Lowther's conviction that Lafayette was one of the men involved in the robbery and murders, Pete Gabriel, who served as both Pinal County Sheriff and US Deputy Marshal, located the runaway suspect in Wheatfields. Wanting Lafayette to admit his part in the crime, the lawman did some fast talking to obtain the young man's confession.

Gabriel informed the inexperienced outlaw that he had witnessed the killing of Hall and saw Lafayette put three bullets in the poor man. Lafayette could not get the words out fast enough. "No, I didn't," he cried. "I only shot him twice." After that, his confession was a mere formality, and he quickly implicated Curtis and Cicero. But he insisted his brother had nothing to do with the murders and only participated in the robbery.

By Wednesday all three men were under arrest. When Sheriff Lowther wired the Wells Fargo agent in San Francisco the culprits had been apprehended but the gold not yet recovered, the agent shot back, "Damn the money. Hang the murderers."

Marshal Gabriel wanted the suspects held in the Florence jail to be tried for tampering with the US mail, but Sheriff Lowther argued the murders of Vail and Hall were more heinous crimes and insisted the men be locked up in Globe. Each of the lawmen may have had his eyes on the reward money, triggering a strong hankering to retain custody of the outlaws. At a deadlock, they finally agreed to let Judge J. D. McCabe determine which charge took precedence, and where the outlaws should be sequestered. The judge ordered the trio remanded into Sheriff Lowther's custody to stand trial for murder.

Tempers were running high in Globe by Wednesday evening. Retaliation for the two murdered men was the conversation running rampant through pristine parlors as well as in smoke-filled saloons. As hot blood permeated the town, Sheriff Lowther ordered all bars closed to allay any drunken violence, but it was too late.

Toward sundown, several hundred angry men assembled outside the jail, ready to break down the door if the sheriff did not turn over the three outlaws. They had already swung three ropes across the big sycamore tree in the middle of town.

Lowther insisted the outlaws receive a fair hearing. He sent for Justice of the Peace George Allen and moved his prisoners to Dr. Stallo's large dancehall, providing sufficient space for almost the entire town to witness the proceedings. Dr. Vail's widow, Irene, was there, along with Cicero's wife, Sylvia, and their four children.

Within minutes Judge Allen determined the prisoners be bound over to Superior Court for trial, but the crowd demanded instant retribution. They had already decided there would be a hanging that night.

Lafayette and Curtis agreed to show the mob where they had stashed the gold, hoping that might improve their dire situation. About thirty men marched the two desperadoes back to Russell Gulch to uncover the hidden treasure.

Meanwhile, Cicero was returned to his cell to await the outcome of the treasure hunt. His life would be spared thanks to the pleas of his wife and Mrs. Vail, both arguing he should be allowed to live since he took no part in the killings.

Returning to town with the loot and the condemned men, the assemblage refused to consider any more delays. As the church bells began to echo across the valley, Lafayette Grime and Curtis Hawley signed confessions and drew up their wills before the throng escorted them down the street to the sycamore tree.

It was now 2:00 a.m. Thursday. Two of the three ropes hanging from the tree were tightened and a dozen burly arms grabbed on to hoist the men to their deaths. Only Lafayette's small, empty boots remained firmly on the ground.

The lifeless bodies remained on the sycamore tree until almost noon before they were finally cut down.

The four-day crime spree resulted in four dead men, one dead mule, and Cicero Grime waiting in fearful expectation that another mob would determine he too should hang.

On September 25, 1882, Cicero was tried and convicted of robbing the US mail and sentenced to serve twenty-one years in Yuma Territorial Prison. He arrived in Yuma on October 11.

The following summer, Cicero started acting mighty strange and his jailers became concerned he would harm himself or someone else with his erratic behavior. Since Arizona would not build a facility for the mentally ill until 1886, prison officials shipped him off to an asylum in Stockton, California.

Two months after his arrival, Cicero walked out of the asylum and was never seen or heard from again. Speculation continues today as to whether he was really insane or faking his madness to get out of prison. In 1884 a man by the name of Robert Alexander was arrested in Oregon and accused of being the long-lost Cicero Grime, but no one could positively say he was the same man who had instigated the robbery in far-off Arizona, and he was released.

Peace returned to Globe until a devastating fire burned a large portion of the town in 1894, including the old sycamore hanging tree. Two years later, what remained of the tree was leveled to the ground. Whiskey-soaked old cowboys will tell you that when the wind whispers across the road where the majestic tree once stood, they can still hear the moans of condemned men who died under the massive sycamore branches. One has to listen hard, however, to hear the cries of Lafayette Grime and Curtis Hawley. They perpetrated their crimes so quickly and so futilely that they barely had time to confess before the tree enveloped them in the throes and satisfaction of vindication.

John Peters Ringo
The Reckless Cowboy

The disheveled man sat peacefully beneath a clump of oak trees, pistol in hand and Winchester rifle propped against a nearby trunk. He made no sound when Misses Morse and Young passed by on the hot afternoon of July 14, 1882, and the two women left the cowboy to sleep off his drunkenness.

A few hours later, wood hauler John Yoast drove his team along this lonely trail near Turkey Creek in the Chiricahua Mountains. He spotted the motionless man and, like Misses Morse and Young, assumed he was asleep. However, his dog would not leave the stranger alone. Yoast took another look at the inebriated soul sprawled on the ground and discovered the lifeless body of John Ringo, a notorious gunslinger known in southeastern Arizona as deadly with a pistol and usually on the wrong side of the law.

Ringo had been lying under the oaks for some time when Yoast came upon him—possibly overnight, as evidenced by the toll the summer heat had already taken on the fetid corpse. Closer examination revealed a bullet hole on the right side of his head and a piece of his scalp missing. The gun in the dead man's hand contained one empty shell.

News of Ringo's death spread across the region faster than a well-aimed bullet. His reputation as a gun-slinging desperado had followed him from Texas and New Mexico into the lawless territory of Arizona, a safe haven for bandits, murderers, and rustlers during the late 1800s.

From the time he arrived in the territory, John Ringo was feared by those who crossed him. He ran with the outlaw Clanton gang—Newman Haynes (Old Man) Clanton and his sons Phineas (Phin), Ike, and Billy—who terrorized southeastern Arizona in the 1880s, rustling cattle and horses, robbing at will, and murdering anyone who got in their way. Ringo also was frequently in dispute with local authorities, often ending up in jail on charges ranging from disturbing the peace to murder.

His family roots gave no indication that he would end up on the wrong side of the law.

Born John Peters Ringo in Wayne County, Indiana, on May 3, 1850, the oldest of five Ringo children, John was thrust early into the role as head of the family. On the trail to California in the summer of 1864, his father's gun accidentally discharged and killed him as fourteen-year-old John looked on helplessly. The shattered family arrived in San Jose in late 1864, but John only stayed a few years before moving on.

He was in Burnett County, Texas, in time for the bloody 1874–75 Mason County War, or Hoodoo War, which was sparked by hatred between German cattle owners in Mason County and American-born cattlemen who lived in adjacent districts. The German contingent had supported the Union during the Civil War, and this led to conflicting factions on the Confederate Texas frontier. The Germans believed local cattlemen were stealing their stock. Ringo sided with the Texas cowhands.

He was implicated in a host of incidents surrounding the Mason County conflict, including a rather innocent incident on Christmas Day 1874, when he was arrested for celebrating the holiday by shooting off his gun in public. But when gambler

James Cheyney showed up dead, Ringo was indicted for the murder. He was also charged with threatening the lives of a sheriff and his deputy.

His incarcerations were a travesty of justice. He was released on a technicality after being tried and convicted on the threat charges. When no witnesses braved the courtroom to testify against him on the murder charges, the case was dismissed.

After Ringo and a band of desperadoes reportedly tried to free a group of men headed for jail, the *Burnet Bulletin* reported, "The notorious Ringo, who seems to have been the leader, is certainly a very desperate and daring man."

Yet by 1878 Ringo seemed to turn his life of crime around when he registered his cattle brand in Mason County and won election as constable in Loyal Valley. The following year, however, he abandoned his Texas holdings and headed for the Arizona desert.

He settled along the border between the Arizona and New Mexico Territories in San Simon Valley and held mining interests in the area. By that December, he was once again on the wrong side of the law. The December 14, 1879, issue of the *Arizona Daily Star* reported:

> Last Tuesday night a shooting took place at Safford in which Louis Hancock was shot by John Ringo. It appears Ringo wanted Hancock to take a drink of whiskey, and he refused saying he would prefer beer. Ringo struck him over the head with his pistol and then fired, the ball taking effect in the lower end of the left ear, and passed through the fleshy part of the neck, half inch more in the neck, would have killed him. Ringo is under arrest. . . . Moral—when you drink with a man that is on a shoot, and he says whiskey, don't you say beer.

Arrested and released on bond, Ringo was scheduled to appear before the Pima County grand jury in March 1880. Days before his scheduled court date, he sent a letter to Tucson Sheriff Charles Shibell explaining he could not make it to town because he had been shot in the foot. The district attorney did not believe a word of Ringo's excuse and had a bench warrant issued for his arrest. Whatever happened in the case of the whiskey versus beer drinking battle went unrecorded.

The following summer, Ringo rode with a gang driving cattle to the San Carlos Indian Reservation. Afterward, the crew members headed into Safford to sop up their thirst at a local saloon.

Abraham Franklin owned a general store in Safford and came to know Ringo well:

> He was about 6 ft. 2 in., light but not a blond with the most pathetic blue eyes I ever saw. A cheerful good looking fellow with a half cynical smile, and a powerful mind. When he said a thing, he meant it and every one knew he meant it. In that was his strength. Of course, he had his pistols, too. He could put up two beer bottles, mouth toward him, let his two pistols hang from his fingers, then with a dexterous jerk, I don't know just how, he would have them in position and break both bottles at once. His main stunt however was shooting from his hip.

Franklin claimed Ringo saved his life on more than one occasion. One incident occurred in Franklin's store when "a crowd was trying to start something . . . Ringo took in the situation at a glance. Stepping up beside me & slamming his gun on the counter, he remarked, 'If there is going to be a row I think I would like to be in on it.' Every one suddenly decided that they had business elsewhere."

Franklin also knew Ringo's darker side. When he drank Franklin said, ". . . you wanted to travel from him like lightening [sic] . . ."

The reckless cowboy again entered politics in August 1880 as one of the Democratic delegates for the San Simon Cienega voting district and attended the Democratic County Convention in Tucson. That October, he was an election official for the San Simon Cienega polling precinct along with cattle rustler Ike Clanton and San Simon rancher A. H. Thompson. But the Pima County Board of Supervisors quickly revoked their candidacy, claiming their residency was in question.

That same year, Ringo partnered with his pal Ike Clanton and filed a ranch claim on 320 acres in Animas Valley, New Mexico Territory. The two planned to run cattle on the land, which they called the Alfalfa or Cienega Ranch.

Nearby, the Arizona silver-mining town of Galeyville had become a refuge for desperadoes who roamed through the territory. With his ranch in close proximity, Ringo frequently hung out in Galeyville, where hard drinking and serious gambling occurred nightly. As one cowboy once remarked, when Ringo was drinking, he was "an over bearing, loud talking, dangerous man."

On a summer night in 1881, Ringo sat in on a game of poker at Evilsinger's saloon in Galeyville. When he ran out of money, he asked if anyone would stake him but all refused. He left disgruntled but returned around midnight with his pal Dave Estes. Guns drawn, Ringo barged through the back door of the saloon while Estes covered the front. They relieved the poker players of about $500 and took off on a stolen horse.

Arrested for the robbery, the twosome pled not guilty. The day of the trial, Ringo showed up, but when no witnesses appeared to testify against him, the hearing was continued until January 1882.

During this time, the legendary O. K. Corral gunfight took place in Tombstone on October 26, 1881. Wyatt Earp tried to finger Ringo as one of the instigators of the melee, but the cowboy was not even in town on that fateful day.

He did appear outside Tombstone's Occidental Saloon on January 17, 1882, meeting up with the dentist Doc Holliday, a close friend of Earp's. Holliday quickly expressed his dislike of Ringo and heated words echoed down the street. Both men caressed the hilts of their guns. Wyatt and Morgan Earp watched with interest as the two men squared off.

The streets were filled with people, so an incident would have certainly injured more than one passerby. Just as the two men stepped back, guns all but drawn, Chief of Police James Flynn confronted Ringo and Holliday, placed them both under arrest, and fined each for carrying a deadly weapon in town. The law in Tombstone at the time required everyone surrender his, or her, weapon upon entering town. Guns were usually deposited with the bartender at the first saloon encountered.

Three days later, Ringo was back in jail for the Galeyville robbery, and he again pled not guilty.

While Ringo lingered in the Tombstone jail, Wyatt Earp and a posse rode out of town supposedly in pursuit of stage robbers and raiders. Earp was actually looking for brothers Ike and Phin Clanton, Ringo's cohorts, as Earp considered them likely culprits in the ambush of Virgil Earp the previous December, just two months after the O. K. Corral escapade.

When Ringo heard about the posse, he asked his attorney to arrange bail so he could ride out to warn his friends of the approaching lawmen. Sheriff John Behan released Ringo. James Earp, Wyatt's brother, saw the desperado galloping out of town and filed an affidavit with the court claiming the thief had escaped.

A second posse headed out to bring back Ringo. Upon arriving in the town of Charleston, the party met Ike Clanton with his pistol drawn. A quick look around town revealed several men on rooftops with rifles aimed at the posse. Clanton argued that Ringo would return to Tombstone on his own terms, and the lawmen agreed to withdraw and wait for the fugitive to show up. Just as promised, Ringo made his way back to Tombstone and back into jail, where he pled not guilty to the Galeyville robbery. He was released on $3,000 bond.

By March 1882, Wyatt Earp and his gang had run amok of the law and were on the lam. Ringo rode with Sheriff Behan and his posse to hunt down Earp after the killing of Florentino Cruz, a hired hand at a wood camp, but the posse never caught up with Earp and his band.

Court convened that May on Ringo's Galeyville robbery charges, but witnesses still refused to come forward, as Ringo was known to extract his own revenge on those who crossed him. All charges were dropped, and Ringo left town. He returned to Tombstone at the beginning of July, staggeringly intoxicated.

A moody, morose Ringo drank heavily for days before meeting up with Samuel Purdy, editor of the *Tombstone Epitaph*. ". . . [H]e was as certain of being killed as he was of living . . .," said Purdy. "He said that he might run along for a couple of years more, and may not last two days."

Six days later, an inebriated, despondent Ringo rode out of Tombstone, headed for the Dragoon Mountains. He had dinner at Dial's Ranch in the south pass of the Dragoons, and on July 9 he arrived in Galeyville, where he continued to consume an abundance of booze. Barely able to stay on his horse, he reeled down the road, bottle in hand, never to be seen alive again.

"His Last Shot. The King of the Cowboys Sends a Bullet Through His Brain," screamed the headline in the *Arizona Daily Star*. The article reported:

> John Ringold [*sic*], one of the best known men in southwestern [*sic*] Arizona was found dead in Morse's Canyon in the Chiricahua mountains last Friday. He evidently committed suicide. He was known in this section as "King of the Cowboys" and was fearless in the extreme. He had many staunch friends and bitter enemies. The pistol with one chamber emptied was found in his clenched fist. He shot himself in the head, the bullet entering on the right side, between the eye and the ear, and coming out on top of the head. . . .

Yet there were those who doubted Ringo had committed suicide, and a handful of reprobates claimed responsibility or were considered viable suspects in his death. Wyatt Earp, who blamed Ringo for the slaying of his brother Morgan and the shooting of Virgil Earp, certainly had motive for killing his archenemy. But Earp had left the Tombstone area over three months prior.

Lady-killer Buckskin Frank Leslie often boasted of killing the drunken cowboy, particularly during his incarceration in Yuma Territorial Prison for the slaying of Blonde Mollie, a singer and dancer at Tombstone's Bird Cage Theater.

And outlaw Mike O'Rourke, alias Johnny-Behind-the-Deuce, is also purported to have pulled the trigger that sent Ringo to his grave.

Over fifty years later, one of the men on the original coroner's panel continued to dispute the claim of murder. He remembered coming upon the body lying on the sun-baked ground: "Blood and brains [were] oozing from the wound and matted his hair. There was an empty shell in the six-shooter and the hammer was on that. I called it suicide fifty-two years ago, I am still calling it suicide."

A third explanation of Ringo's death might be that the roaring drunk cowboy accidentally shot and killed himself. As he made his way through the mountains, Ringo was as sotted as any man could be and still sit on a horse. He continued to drink as he bobbed along the trail. Somewhere along the way he got off his horse, removed his boots, and for some reason tied an undershirt around his feet. His horse left him as he sat under the oak trees to finish his bottle of whiskey. He wore two cartridge belts and may have taken them off while he rested, as one of his belts was buckled upside down when his body was found.

Maybe something spooked him as he sought the shade of the oak trees. He was known to have a deep-seated fear of being killed, which might have made him so leery in his drunken state that he pulled his pistol to defend himself from whatever imagined horror was stalking him. A twig snap or a ripple from nearby Turkey Creek could have set him off. He might have fallen and shot himself as he dropped to the ground, battering his head on one of the trees as he collapsed. If he died instantly, his gun might never have left his hand.

John Peters Ringo
Courtesy of the Arizona Historical Society/Tucson, AHS #78486

According to the coroner's report, no powder burns were found on the body. This led to the supposition that Ringo had been killed by an unknown assailant. But Ringo had been sitting in the hot sun for hours with his body rapidly decomposing and turning black, quite possibly obliterating any traces of gunpowder markings.

The coroner was no help in determining how John Ringo died; he cautiously listed the cause of death as "unknown but presumed from gunshot wounds."

Unlike most cowboys who vow to be buried with their boots on, John Ringo lies shoeless behind the cluster of oak trees that shaded him from the hot July sun that fateful day when he died alone, bleary-eyed and possibly paralyzed with fear. The *Tombstone Epitaph* ran a lengthy, detailed account of his death, concluding, "Many friends will mourn him, and many others will take secret delight in learning of his death."

James Addison Reavis
The Noble Forger

Imagine walking into the capital of Arizona and demanding ownership of more than twelve million acres of land spanning 235 miles west to east from Phoenix to the western boundaries of Silver City, New Mexico , and seventy-five miles north and south encompassing not only the Phoenix population but dozens of outlying agricultural and mining communities including Tempe, Mesa, Casa Grande, Florence, Safford, Globe, Miami, Superior, Clifton, Coolidge, and Morenci.

Five rivers run through this massive desert region and just as many Indian reservations occupy territory within its boundaries. The San Francisco and Mogollon Mountains jut out the eastern portion of the expanse with the Picacho, Galiuro, and Pinaleno Mountain ranges spanning the southern end.

Military enclaves fall within these boundaries and railroads run across the territory. Thousands of people occupy the land. Some claim less than an acre while others hold deeds to hundreds of acres that they farm, ranch, and mine. About 125 years ago, James Addison Reavis sought to claim all this land and everything that was on it as his own, and he almost got away with it.

Reavis was already in his thirties when he arrived in Arizona in 1880, but he had not been idle during his formative years. A Missourian by birth, he joined the Confederate Army at the age of eighteen but found military life dull and uninteresting. To keep himself occupied he practiced forging his commanding

41

officer's signature and was soon handing out bogus leave papers and furloughs to his army buddies. When his ruse was discovered, he headed across the Mason-Dixon Line and enlisted in the Union Army. Boredom overtook him again. He asked for an official leave to marry and left the military, never to return.

Young Reavis spent a year in Brazil before settling in St. Louis, Missouri, around 1865 where he worked as a conductor on horse-drawn streetcars. He invested his meager earnings in land and property, never hesitating to produce a missing deed or document by falsifying the necessary papers. Soon his proclivity for fraud and forgery brought devious businessmen to his door, and he gladly created counterfeit papers for those willing to pay for his talent.

In 1871 Dr. George M. Willing Jr. came looking for Reavis. Willing had abandoned his wife and children in St. Louis some years back to seek his fortune in the lucrative western goldfields. He claimed he had purchased a large tract of land in Arizona Territory from Miguel Peralta and his father, descendants of Spanish nobility who were now living in poverty. It was rich land, ripe for farming and ranching, and, according to his calculations, a wealth of gold and silver lay beneath the rocky soil. Would Reavis be interested in entering into a partnership to develop this valuable property?

Reavis listened intently as Dr. Willing described the bounty that awaited in Arizona. Whether he believed Willing or not, he saw opportunity far beyond what the good doctor envisioned and readily entered into the partnership. Willing headed west in late 1873. Reavis tarried long enough to marry Ada Pope on May 5, 1874, but left shortly thereafter and did not see Ada again for over six years. She divorced him in 1883, claiming desertion.

Reavis's route took him through the Isthmus of Panama into California. He arrived in San Francisco only to discover Willing had died in Prescott, Arizona, in March 1874. Willing's unclaimed gunnysack of belongings, including the deeds he said he had acquired from the Peralta heirs, was stowed in the coroner's attic in Prescott.

Reavis stayed in California for several years and taught school in Downey before hiring on as a subscription agent with the *San Francisco Daily Examiner*. During this time, he formulated a convoluted plan to make the best of his deal with the deceased Willing.

Reavis took the meager information Willing had related to him and set about creating a dynasty of enormous proportions. He knew that under the terms of the Treaty of Guadalupe Hidalgo (1848) and the Gadsden Purchase (1854), the United States was obligated to recognize valid Spanish and Mexican land grants. Most of the Arizona grants were considered worthless and had been abandoned by the original owners.

By now Reavis must have doubted that Miguel Peralta and his father even existed. Or if they did, they were far from the noble inheritors Willing had proclaimed them to be. He had seen enough forged documents in his day to figure out that the papers Willing had shown him were worthless. But those official-looking certificates, now reposing in the attic of the Prescott coroner's office, would become the impetus upon which he planned to defraud the people of Arizona out of millions of acres of land, and they must be dealt with. He had to obtain clear title to continue with his devious plot.

The Peralta Grant, as he decided to call his acreage, would become property bequeathed to the family by proclamation of the King of Spain. Now all he had to do was create the Peralta clan, falsify existing records, and deposit these fraudulent documents where they could be "discovered" as evidence of the family's legal right to the land.

The family Reavis concocted began its reign in Spain in 1708 with the birth of Don Miguel Nemecio Silva de Peralta de la Córdoba. Don Miguel entered the service of the King of Spain and was sent to Guadalajara in New Spain (now Mexico) as a city inspector. Reavis gave him the title the Baron of Arizonaca and had the king bestow upon him a grant of land.

Don Miguel, according to Reavis, visited his northern tract of land only once, declaring the area around what is now Casa Grande the Barony of Arizona. Murderous Apaches purportedly drove him out of the region back to Mexico.

Don Miguel did not marry until he was sixty-two years old, Reavis claimed, but he soon had a son, Jesus Miguel Silva de Peralta de la Córdoba y Sanches de Bonilla, born in 1781. To eliminate the need for another generation, Reavis allowed Don Miguel to live to the age of 116. When he died, all his property went to Jesus Miguel. Under Reavis's penmanship, Jesus Miguel became the father of the miner who sold the Peralta lands to Dr. Willing. The Peraltas seemed to have long lifelines.

Reavis now had to get his hands on the deeds Willing had shown him in St. Louis.

When he stepped off the stagecoach in Phoenix in 1880, Reavis passed himself off as a reporter for the *Examiner*. Dressed in a long black coat and carrying a silver-knobbed cane, the tall, imposing man with sapphire blue eyes and a startling shock of red hair set out almost immediately for Prescott to locate the gunnysack Willing had left behind. He found the bag filled with Willing's clothing and odd items. At the very bottom lay the deeds signed by father and son, Jesus and Miguel Peralta. Reavis had only one more person to eliminate in order to claim the Peralta property as his own.

Mary Ann Willing had known Reavis in St. Louis and trusted his friendship without reservation. When Reavis promised her thousands of dollars if she would sign over to him her late husband's interest in the Peralta documents, she did not hesitate. Now with complete control of the false Peralta Grant, Reavis set about producing the documents he believed would convince the government of Arizona that the land grant actually existed.

With his penmanship expertise, he spent weeks perfecting forged documents. He re-created inks used in the 1700s and painstakingly practiced writing with the flourish of old Spanish monks and scribes. When he was satisfied with his masterpieces, he traveled to Spain and Mexico, surreptitiously inserting these well-crafted, ancient-looking papers into church records and official depositories verifying the existence of the Peralta family. At the same time, he furtively filched documents that disproved the existence of this noble clan.

All this planning and scheming took an enormous amount of time, effort, expertise, lying, cheating, and counterfeiting before Reavis felt he had established the Peralta lineage. By 1882 he was ready to lay claim to twelve million acres of prime Arizona land.

The man with the well-manicured mustache and sweeping sideburns who appeared in Tucson in March 1882 carried a suitcase brimming with "authentic" documents. He quickly hustled down the road to the Graham County courthouse in Safford to file papers asserting his legal ownership by purchase of the Peralta Grant. When the court refused to recognize his claim, Reavis returned to California to manufacture even more documents. In March 1883 he was back in Tucson filing a raft of deeds, documents, photographs, and conveyances with the US surveyor general, claiming himself the rightful landowner to the twelve-million-acre Peralta Grant.

Reavis wasted no time collecting from those he insisted were usurping his land. He sold quitclaims to nervous farmers, ranchers, and settlers who were fearful of losing property they believed they already owned. They worried that if Reavis was the rightful owner, they would never obtain clear titles to their homes and properties unless they gave in to his demands. He requested little money from these small landowners and often, for the price of a meal, he would give away a quitclaim or two. His purpose was to show that by signing the deeds, the good citizens of Arizona recognized his legal right to the land. Many were skeptical and refused to sign, but Reavis persevered in his quest for his "rightful" and "legal" property.

After it was reported the Southern Pacific Railroad had capitulated to his demands and agreed to pay $50,000 to continue building tracks across his property, Reavis felt he had the Territory of Arizona up against a wall. But the papers he had filed with the surveyor general were under careful scrutiny.

In 1885 the court determined Reavis's claim was invalid. Tempers mounted against the stately gentleman. He fled to San Francisco with the *Weekly Phoenix Herald* proclaiming him the ". . . Earl of the Iron Jaw, Count of Confidence Land, Lord of the Limber Tongue and Great Mogul of the Territory. . . . Cheek thy name is Reavis!" He did not return for two years.

James Addison Reavis, "The Baron of Arizona"
Courtesy of Arizona Historical Society/Tucson, AHS #B112040

Reavis determined he needed a direct Peralta descendant to convince the courts the grant existed. He found his "angel" on the streets of California and transformed her into the Baroness of Arizona.

Sophia Treadway was born around 1864 to John and Kate Treadway, but they were long gone from her life when she ran into the devious Reavis. He sent her to a convent to learn how to behave like a lady and educate her in the refinements of royalty. In 1887 he introduced her to Tucson society as Doña Sophia Micaela Maso Reavis y Peralta de la Córdoba, his wife.

Reavis had to concoct the story of Doña Sophia's pedigree and place her within the Peralta dynasty. His fictional narrative proclaimed she was the great-granddaughter of the first Baron of Arizona. She had been born a twin but her brother died at birth and her mother shortly thereafter. She was raised in Mendocino County, California, by her grandmother. Reavis said he first laid eyes on Doña Sophia while on a train and he immediately recognized her ancestral features as belonging to the Peralta clan.

When he was satisfied he had established Doña Sophia's royal birth, Reavis got out his ink pen to create the documents perfecting her lineage.

He set off once again on his well-traveled route to Spain and Mexico, leaving his newly crafted papers in the same depositories he had previously visited. When he returned to the states, he revealed documents "miraculously" found proving his wife's heritage, including the old will of Jesus Miguel bequeathing all his holdings, and particularly the Peralta land, to his granddaughter Doña Sophia.

In September 1887 Reavis, now calling himself James Addison Peralta-Reavis, filed the previously missing will with the Tucson office of the surveyor general. The *Arizona Daily Citizen* lamented, "It seems as if the woes of Arizona were never to end. First come the Apaches and then the blackmailers and land grabbers."

"Everything that I have done has been in the interest of my wife and not for any claim preferred by me," Reavis told the *San Francisco Examiner.* "I have nothing to do with it except in my character as her [Doña Sophia's] husband. It is my duty to see that her rights are given her, and you can rest assured that I intend doing it."

While Reavis was busily counterfeiting, filching, and inserting the documents necessary to establish his argument that the Peralta Grant existed, Royal Johnson, the territory's Surveyor General, was working diligently to disprove the validity of the reams of papers filed by Reavis. In 1889 he reported his findings noting that many of Reavis's documents were written with a steel pen, an instrument not used until after 1800. He accurately pointed out the differences in penmanship between authenticated documents written in the 1700s and those filed by Reavis purportedly written at the same time. Paper watermarks appeared that were not available until the mid-1800s. There were misspellings of Spanish words in some of the fraudulent documents. Johnson ordered a search of Spanish archives for papers pertaining to the Peralta claim and found no evidence of the family. His report concluded with a recommendation that Reavis's claim be denied, "it being in my mind without the slightest foundation in fact and utterly void."

Reavis filed suit against the government, seeking damages of $10 million. He said the monies already paid to him proved the validity of his claim. Along with the Southern Pacific Railroad's $50,000, the Silver King Mining Company had handed over $25,000. In all, Reavis had already collected more than $145,000 from landowners for the rights to use Peralta land, a sum equivalent to over $3 million today.

Reavis brought his claim before the newly formed Court of Private Land Claims (established in 1891) in Santa Fe, New Mexico.

When court convened on June 3, 1895, Reavis was nowhere to be found, nor did he appear the next day, but the trial went forth without him. On June 5 the court received a telegram from Reavis asking the trial be continued until June 10.

Finally appearing and placed on the stand, Reavis proclaimed his sole desire in attaining the Peralta Grant was "to develop Arizona. As a fact, I never cared that much for the grant, except the honor of having done something in it. I am not a lover of money, but I am a lover of development and building up a country. Therefore my whole life has been in the interest of building up Arizona . . ."

For two and a half days, he rambled on about the Peralta family. Then he wheeled a large truck into the courtroom that he claimed contained absolute proof of his wife's heritage. He began pulling copious amounts of documents out of the truck. Next came dozens of portraits, pictures of his wife's ancestors, he said. He argued this was all the proof the court should require to award his wife her rightful property. This was most likely the evidence he was creating during his absence from court.

The court did not believe a word he said. His claim was deemed "wholly fictitious and fraudulent," and he was immediately arrested and charged with conspiracy to defraud the government.

James Addison Reavis in prison
Courtesy of Arizona State Library, Archives and Public Records, History and Archives Division,
#97-7968

Unable to provide bail, Reavis languished in jail for more than a year. His criminal trial commenced on June 27, 1896, and lasted just a few short days. Much of the same testimony presented at the first trial was again introduced. Witnesses who had initially backed Reavis's story now admitted they had lied. He was found "guilty as charged in the indictment to default the United States government out of parts of its public lands in connection with the effort to establish the fictitious and fraudulent Peralta Grant."

Reavis's sentence was rather mild considering he had hoped to acquire a good portion of Arizona Territory with his fraudulent scheme. He was sentenced to serve two years in the Santa Fe Penitentiary and pay a fine of $5,000. He promised he would appeal his conviction but never did. On April 18, 1898, he walked out of prison proclaiming he would once again "return to the world of business."

His wife, now using the name Sophia Treadway Reavis, and no longer asserting her noble status, settled in Denver with the couple's twin boys, Miguel and Carlos, born in 1893, and their adopted son, Fenton. In 1902 she filed for divorce, citing desertion and nonsupport.

Reavis languished in California, never again experiencing the opulent lifestyle he enjoyed as an Arizona aristocrat. Penniless, he took up residency in the Los Angeles County Poor Farm but moved to Denver in 1914. He died on November 20, 1914.

No other criminal came close to robbing Arizona of the vast sums of money and millions of acres of land that James Addison Reavis tried to swindle. He was a brilliant and talented man who lived a life of fraud and fantasy. His scheme to be acknowledged as a nobleman earned him only one thing, the dubious title of the Baron of Arizona.

Charles P. Stanton
The Puppetmaster

The eight desperadoes rose from the desert floor like a deadly mirage in the torrid July heat, descending on the lone wagon as it made its way along the sun-baked road. With little fanfare they grabbed the driver and stabbed him to death as his family watched in horror. As the mother and her two young sons frantically pleaded for their lives, a bald-headed man with no eyebrows or eyelashes grabbed the woman by the hair and held her head back while another quickly slit her throat. Within seconds the boys met the same fate. Wasting no time, the men methodically scalped their victims, tossed the bodies into the wagon, confiscated a strongbox, and set fire to the carriage, obliterating all traces of the Barney Martin family.

From a nearby hilltop a man watched as the massacre went down, the smell of burning flesh not at all unpleasant to him. An evil smirk played across his smarmy face as the eight men rode up the hill and dropped the strongbox at his feet. Taking his share of the loot, Charles P. Stanton headed back to Antelope Station, a small mining community near Wickenburg, Arizona. He stashed his plunder in a secluded spot, poured himself a glass of the finest Irish whiskey, and toasted his success. He had just masterminded a reprehensible crime without getting any blood on his lily-white hands.

When the remains of the Martin family were found on August 8, 1886, almost three weeks after they had disappeared, only a few bone fragments were left to bury.

Charles P. Stanton, the man who had instigated this atrocious crime, preferred the title Lord Stanton, claiming he was the son of an Irish aristocrat. Of course there is no proof of his lineage, just as there would be no proof he perpetrated some of the vilest offenses in Arizona history.

As a young man, Stanton attended Dublin's Trinity College and entered Monmouth Monastery in England to study for the priesthood. However, he was expelled from Monmouth, either for stealing from the coffers or for immoral acts. Whatever the reason, he departed England for America with a bounty of £1,000 on his head.

Few records exist of Stanton's first few years in the United States, but he was probably in his mid-thirties when he filed for US citizenship in New York City in 1864. By the time his petition was granted on August 26, 1872, he was already creating a westward path of destruction.

He may have been involved in the John Slack and Philip Arnold Diamond Hoax that erupted across the country in 1872. Two prospectors had liberally salted the Wyoming hills with inferior diamonds and rubies and passed them off as valuable precious stones just waiting to be plucked from the ground. Wealthy, intelligent people spent millions of dollars investing in this fraudulent scheme, never believing a couple of destitute miners could outsmart them. Some believe Stanton may have gotten his hands on a sizeable amount of the profits from this venture. No proof exists of his involvement, but chances are, he was running from the law when he arrived in Arizona Territory in the early 1870s.

Charles Stanton standing outside his store
Courtesy of Sharlot Hall Museum Library and Archives, Prescott, Arizona, #BU-B-8097P

He went to work as an assayer and gemologist for Sexton White, owner of the Vulture Mine near Wickenburg. After the mine closed, he continued to analyze prospectors' ore findings, usually with some of the gold dust ending up in his pocket and the miner no wiser than a blind owl.

Stanton settled in Antelope Station at the base of Rich Hill, where one of the richest deposits of placer gold was discovered in 1863. Prospectors dug out more than 10,000 gold nuggets in just a few months and the mountain continued to yield its wealth over the next few years. By the time Stanton showed up, however, the mountaintop had little left to offer. Miners still clung to the hope of finding another big lode, but most turned to farming and ranching for their livelihoods. Antelope Creek and the nearby Hassayampa River provided ample nourishment for crops and cattle.

Pioneer ranchers Charles and Ida Genung, well respected in the Wickenburg area, were impressed with the sophisticated and knowledgeable assayer and welcomed Stanton into their home to educate their three daughters. It was not long, however, before the girls complained their new tutor touched them inappropriately. Never one to waste words or actions, Ida grabbed her pistol and ordered the Irishman out of her house never to return. From then on, Charles Genung kept a close watch over Stanton's dealings.

By 1875 Antelope Station contained a five-stamp mill, a boardinghouse, and about a dozen houses. A post office was established with Stanton elected postmaster, although many of the names that showed up on the election ballots were also found on nearby gravestones, leading many to suspect the new postmaster had rigged the polls. Before long he had also accepted the duties of deputy sheriff and justice of the peace, then proceeded to rename the town. Antelope Station became known as Stanton, Arizona Territory. The new name lasted about six months before voters were able to reestablish the community as Antelope Station.

Two men ran rival stage stops and stores in the bustling township, competing for business from stagecoaches traveling to and from Phoenix, Prescott, and the Colorado River towns. Storeowner Yaqui Wilson endeared himself to hungry passengers by raising his own beef and hogs and preparing hearty meals greedily devoured after a tedious journey. Plus, his home-brewed whiskey, well known and desired throughout the territory, was always a thirst-quencher after a dusty ride. But when the stage company added a barn to house and feed its horses near Englishman William Partridge's place, coaches no longer stopped at Wilson's establishment. Passengers, however, preferring Wilson's food to Partridge's less-than-edible vittles, often got off at Partridge's and walked the half-mile to Wilson's to eat. There was no love lost between the two men.

Stanton also set up a general store, but most people preferred to avoid the often rude and offensive shopkeeper. What Stanton really wanted was the lucrative stagecoach business benefiting the other two establishments. Befriending both men, he devised a malevolent scheme to eliminate his competition.

Whoever let Yaqui Wilson's hogs loose knew exactly where they would head. The porkers loved the bucknut shrubbery and prickly pear fruit that covered William Partridge's property. However, the swine did not know the outside from the inside and invaded Partridge's house, creating a considerable mess. Aware of the escalating feud between the two men, Stanton judiciously advised Wilson to apologize to Partridge for his hogs' behavior and to pay for what had been ruined. Out of the other side of his mouth, he informed Partridge that Wilson was out to kill him.

Rifle in hand, Partridge met up with the apologetic Wilson and shot him before the poor man could utter a word. When Partridge realized Wilson had come to him unarmed, he fled into the desert. Following the fugitive, Stanton persuaded Partridge to turn himself in. At the trial Stanton testified against the woeful Englishman, solidifying the poor man's conviction for second-degree murder. On November 2, 1877, Partridge was sentenced to life in the Yuma Territorial Prison.

With his two rivals now out of the way, Stanton became the most powerful man in Antelope Station. He was ready to step in and take over the two businesses abandoned by the death of Wilson and incarceration of Partridge. But Wilson had a partner, John Timmerman, who decided to run the dead man's store. Partridge's creditors hired Barney Martin to run the other station. Stanton was furious he had lost out on these two lucrative holdings and decided he needed more muscle.

Francisco Vega (or Valenzuela), a big, ugly man with little hair anywhere on his head, led a band of desperadoes who enjoyed a reign of terror over central Arizona, looting and killing at will. They made their headquarters in Weaver, a nearby ramshackle mining settlement that catered to renegades and criminals. Travelers, fearing for their lives, often avoided this part of the country. Stanton hired the malevolent outlaws whenever he needed a particularly cruel or vindictive deed accomplished. He decided to use their expertise against his competitors.

The inexperienced Timmerman had gratefully accepted Stanton's offer to assist him with the store's books, so when Timmerman set out for Wickenburg one day, he told Stanton he had $700 in gold dust with him to pay off a San Francisco merchant. As Timmerman sauntered down the dusty road to Wickenburg, Juan Reval, one of Vega's men, suddenly appeared beside him. With little conversation between the two men, Reval shot Timmerman through the heart, relieved him of the gold he carried, doused the body in oil, and set it on fire. Stanton watched the slaying from a safe distance. He and Reval split the proceeds of the heist, adding to Stanton's blood-money stash. There was absolutely no evidence linking Stanton to the crime.

Appointing himself appraiser of Timmerman's estate, Stanton also named himself the storeowner's sole beneficiary. He had accomplished half of what he set out to do. Now only the Martin family stood in his way.

When Barney Martin started receiving death threats, he initially dismissed them as pranks. Then his barn burned down, and soon after his house lay in a heap of smoldering cinders. He rebuilt the house, but as he again watched it go up in flames, he saw Stanton running from the fire. Grabbing his rifle, Martin took aim but his gun had been tampered with and did not go off. Disgusted and distraught, he knew he had to get his family out of harm's way. Martin sold his property for $5,000 and set out that hot July day in 1886 for a new beginning in Phoenix.

The two-day trip was eased by an overnight visit with friends, and Martin expected Charles Genung to accompany him on the road into Phoenix. Genung had been delayed on business, however, and never met up with the Martins. As Martin steered his horses along the well-rutted road, Mrs. Martin kept her eye on their two boys, ages nine and eleven, bouncing about in the rear of the wagon, their clothes covered in layers of road dust. She despaired of ever getting them clean again.

Stanton knew Martin carried the money from the sale of his property. As one of Vega's men later confessed, Stanton hired the outlaws to eliminate the Martin family, insisting they make the massacre look like the work of raiding Indians. Elano Hernandez, one of the vilest men to walk the earth, ordered Martin out of the wagon and slit his throat before Martin could grab his gun.

Genung knew Stanton was behind the killings and would not let the investigation rest in the hands of lawmen who were under the Irishman's control. As his grandson, Dan B. Genung, later wrote, his grandfather went to see Mrs. McGinnis, who often cooked for the Vega gang. She claimed the killers got drunk one night and bragged about the murders. They laughed, she said, when they described how Mrs. Martin, who had often cared for

Vega's wife and four children, pleaded with the outlaws to spare her and her two youngsters. As she clung to his knees begging for their lives, Vega thanked the distraught woman for her kindness to his family, then grabbed her hair so Hernandez could slit her throat. The boys soon lay beside their mother. The outlaws' only disappointment, said Mrs. McGinnis, was that Genung was not with the Martin family as expected. Stanton wanted Genung out of the way as the rancher had become too suspicious of the Irishman's covert activities.

Stanton reveled in the authority and power he now held over the town. Even the *Tombstone Epitaph* described the little burg as "bloody Stanton." Disasters haunted the district, but no one could touch Lord Stanton.

After a rancher refused to buy supplies from the Irishman's store because his prices were too high, the cattleman found himself watching helplessly as his property went up in flames. A safe distance away, Stanton warmed himself from the heat of the fire.

Two cattlemen caught Francisco Vega trying to set fire to their ranch house. They lectured the outlaw, told him never to come near their property again, and let him go. Shortly a large grass fire forced the ranchers to relocate more than fourteen hundred head of cattle hundreds of miles away in Tombstone. Vega and Stanton enjoyed a good laugh and a stiff drink as the cowboys herded their cattle out of town.

Back in 1870 Dennis May had discovered the profitable Leviathon gold mine. Stanton told May not to worry about filing the proper yearly paperwork to keep the mine in May's name. As justice of the peace, he would handle it. But Stanton never filed the annual assessments and eventually threatened to report May if the prospector did not give up half interest in one of the most lucrative gold mines in the district. An irate May was so disgusted over his forced partnership with Stanton that he sold his remaining interest in the mine for a mere $10,000.

About the same time the Martin family disappeared, E. O. Grant's store in Wickenburg almost went up in flames when someone threw a flaming ball of oil-saturated cotton through the shed window where several barrels of oil and liquor were stored. Tracks led to the Vulture Mill and then toward Stanton's place.

Charles Genung also experienced Stanton's vindictiveness when one of his houses burned down.

Stanton's most heinous crimes, however, occurred when young girls crossed his path. More than one bore the marks of his brutality, while others disappeared after run-ins with the debaucher. Fourteen-year-old Froilano Lucero survived a vile attack perpetrated by Stanton. Her brothers set out to avenge their sister's honor.

Pedro Lucero and his brother watched one day as the burly Stanton headed down the road. Pedro took aim and fired, his bullet nicking the Irishman's ear. His brother missed altogether. Irate over the attack, Stanton offered a $5,000 reward for Pedro, dead or alive. He also issued warrants for the entire town of Weaver, certain he would catch some of the Lucero family in his net. When he could not locate his ear-piercing enemy, he swore out a warrant for Pedro's father. Under Stanton's orders, deputies arrested the frail sixty-year-old and beat him senseless as they escorted him into Prescott and locked him up. He was eventually released when Genung paid his bail.

In September 1886 Juan Reval, serving time on an unrelated charge, confessed he had murdered John Timmerman on Stanton's orders. He also admitted his part in a stage robbery that netted three gold bars, one of which ended up in Stanton's hands. Already the prime suspect behind the Martin murders after another of Vega's men, an Indian, confessed to following Stanton's orders in the brutal attack, Lord Stanton was arrested and taken to Phoenix. But the testimony of a convicted felon and an Indian outlaw were not enough to keep him behind bars. No concrete evidence materialized linking Stanton with any of the crimes of which he was accused and he was released. He boldly rode out of town on one of Barney Martin's horses.

On the evening of November 13, 1886, as he often did on a Saturday night, Stanton closed the door of his store and offered a drink to one of his cronies named Kelly (or Kelley). As they nipped at their whiskey, they heard horses ride up. Three men stood politely in the doorframe requesting directions to Walnut Grove and asking if they could camp nearby for the night. They also wanted to buy some tobacco. Stanton invited the men inside and went behind the counter to retrieve the smokes. As he turned toward the men, one of them aimed straight at Stanton's heart and did not miss.

The three Lucero brothers fled as Kelly opened fire; one never made it out of the yard. Some say Kelly killed the man while others believe he was hit with a bullet from one of his own brothers' guns.

No one bothered to investigate, much less arrest, the individuals who had ended the life of Charles P. Stanton. Everyone sighed with relief and gave thanks Lord Stanton was no longer the aristocratic puppetmaster who controlled the strings of power in the tiny hamlet of Antelope Station.

News also spread that Francisco Vega, the bald-headed man with no soul, had escaped into Mexico, although Charles

Genung later heard the outlaw had been gunned down near Wickenburg running from a stagecoach robbery.

In 1895 mining engineer George Upton bought the town of Antelope Station, but its population was declining rapidly. For unknown reasons in 1896, the community voted to return the town's name to Stanton. As the Great Depression raged across the country in the late 1920s, the mining community experienced a small revival when dozens of out-of-work, hungry men set up lean-to shacks and tents and tried to eke out a living working old placers.

Over the years the old post office opened and closed as often as a saloon door. Shut down in 1890 it reopened in 1894. By 1905 the town fell into a permanent downhill demise and the post office was officially discontinued. The town never again experienced the days when gold and Charles P. Stanton were its masters.

In 1959 Upton's niece, who had acquired the town after her uncle's death, sold part of Stanton to the *Saturday Evening Post* magazine to be used as the grand prize in a jingle contest. The rest of the town was eventually sold to the Lost Dutchman Mining Association.

Today Charles Stanton's legacy can be found scattered among a few old adobe buildings, an infinite assortment of prickly pear cactus, overgrown weeds, languishing desert blooms, and a scattering of tombstones. Stanton's grave, however, lies about a mile outside of town in a desolate canyon circled by watchful vultures. He is not wanted in the town that bears his name.

The Apache Kid
Army Scout, Apache Rebel

On May 3, 1887, the earth trembled across southwestern United States territory and northern Mexico. The earthquake, estimated at about 7.2 magnitude, lasted a full minute with massive rocks careening down mountains and huge fissures dashing jaggedly across the desert terrain, sending adobe homes crashing to the ground. Newspapers reported "deep rumblings" in the desert near the town of Superior, Arizona, where ". . . large pieces of rock were detached on all sides of Picket Post Mountain . . . raising a cloud of dust, and for several minutes it ascended about the mountain giving it the appearance of a live volcano."

About twenty miles east of Superior, Apache Indians, forced to live on the San Carlos Indian Reservation, believed earthquakes foretold the onset of doom and disaster. To alleviate their fears, they gathered to brew *tizwin*, a potent, fermented mixture combining the heart of the maguey or mescal plant with fruits and vegetables. The ensuing *tizwin* party altered the lives of many Apaches that day, but the life of Haskay-bay-nay-ntayl, known to Anglos as the Apache Kid, or Kid for short, was changed beyond redemption.

A trusted Indian scout with the white man's army on the San Carlos Indian Reservation, the Apache Kid knew his people were forbidden to brew the intoxicating *tizwin*, but as he was mourning the slaying of his father, Toga-de-Chuz, he joined the illegal gathering. Toga-de-Chuz's murderer, Gon-zizzie, had been killed by Toga-de-Chuz's friends. As the eldest son, Kid was expected to avenge his father's death in his own way.

Kid drank his share of the liquor and was soon plotting to kill Rip, the brother of Gon-zizzie. He enlisted his half brother, As-ki-say-la-ha, who was also an Indian scout, and the two rode off to roust three more scouts before setting out to find Rip.

Rip stood no chance against Kid's precise aim—he was dead before he hit the ground. Their mission a success, Kid and the four scouts returned to the reservation. They had been gone without permission for five days. Al Sieber, chief of the Indian scouts, had been looking for his wayward men.

For the most part, Sieber managed his troop of Indian scouts with an iron hand and a compassionate heart, but trouble spewed across his face when the scraggly group appeared before him. Sieber demanded their weapons and Kid was the first to obey. A crowd gathered as Sieber ordered the men arrested and locked in the guardhouse—a smelly, bug-infested hole furnished with only a handful of straw and a bucket.

Suddenly shots rang out from the crowd and Sieber, unarmed, fell to the ground with a bullet embedded in his ankle. Seizing the opportunity, Kid grabbed a horse and fled the ensuing melee. He did not intend to lose his freedom for avenging his father's death, something he was compelled to do according to Apache law. As he turned his back on the white man's rules and laws, his days as a trusted Indian scout were over.

Has-kay-bay-nay-ntayl was born around 1860 near the Aravaipa Canyon in eastern Arizona. A loose translation of his name, "brave and tall and will come to a mysterious end," seemed to predict his calamitous future.

Has-kay-bay-nay-ntayl was forced onto the San Carlos Indian Reservation, as were many Indians, through the actions of President Ulysses S. Grant, who established San Carlos in 1872. The government determined the only way to control warring Apaches was to confine them to reservations where they were expected to raise crops instead of raiding nearby ranches. Has-kay-bay-nay-ntayl's father was a member of Capitán Chiquito's band of White Mountain Apaches, who in 1875 were herded onto the dry, desolate reservation aptly called "Hell's Forty Acres."

As a teenager, Has-kay-bay-nay-ntayl seemed to adapt to reservation living. He learned to speak English and shunned the traditional dress of his father, opting to wear suit jackets, felt hats, and leather boots—white man's clothing. On the reservation he was in charge of shooting cattle as they came into the pens for slaughter and he became an expert marksman by running along fence lines surrounding the cattle pens while taking dead aim on the doomed creatures. He also herded cattle for ranchers in the nearby town of Globe. Because Anglos found his Apache name too hard to pronounce, they dubbed him Kid.

Around 1879 Al Sieber made this cocky nineteen-year-old his orderly and cook. With Sieber's encouragement Kid enlisted as an Indian scout in 1881 and reenlisted seven times until 1887. He often took time off between reenlistments, and during one of these respites, he married and fathered a child.

The military quickly promoted Kid to first sergeant, a rank he held during most of his enlistment, when they discovered how accurately he could spot distant riders and decipher whether they were whites or Indians. He was considered better than any military posse at tracking down runaway Indians, and Sieber often relied on him to help train new Indian scouts.

In 1882 he fought in the Battle of Big Dry Wash on the Tonto Rim near the town of Payson, and he accompanied Sieber into Mexico during the 1885 Geronimo campaign.

He did not always toe the military line, however. In Mexico in late 1885, he almost got himself killed when he and two other scouts were accused of molesting a Mexican woman. As the scouts fled, shots rang out—one dead, one wounded, and Kid arrested. Mexican authorities, fearing an international incident if they tried the scout, released him back to the States after charging him a fine of twenty-five dollars.

When Sieber departed San Carlos for Fort Apache on an inspection trip just before that fateful day in May 1887, he left Kid in charge of the scouts. *Tizwin* and trouble soon merged into the incident that found the Apache Kid a renegade outlaw hunted by the very scouts he had trained.

About a dozen rebels fled the reservation along with Kid, and his band increased in numbers as days turned into weeks. When two ranchers were found dead near Benson, their cattle butchered and horses long gone, word spread that the runaway Indians were the culprits.

As the posse closed in, the Apaches surrendered.

On June 25, 1887, Kid and the four Indian scouts who had ridden with him to avenge his father's death were tried for mutiny and desertion in a general court-martial. Kid wasted no time admitting his guilt:

> I am 1st Sergeant Kid, San Carlos, Arizona Territory.
> God sent bad spirit in my heart, I think. You all know all
> the people can't get along very well in the world. There
> are some good people and some bad people amongst
> them all. I am not afraid to tell all these things because

I have not done very much harm. I killed one man
whose name is Rip because he killed my father. I am not
educated like you and therefore can't say very much. If I
had made any arrangement before I came in, I would not
have given up my arms at Mr. Sieber's tent. That is all I
have to say.

At the end of the day, all five scouts were found guilty and
sentenced to death by shooting. After military commander General Nelson A. Miles reviewed the case, he requested leniency for
the men, arguing they were "ignorant, unlettered Indians . . .,"
and while their deeds were certainly serious, they were "not of
that extreme gravity which would justify the death sentence."
The same court that had condemned them to death reduced
their sentences to life in prison at Fort Leavenworth, Kansas.

For six months the Indians languished in the fetid San Carlos
jail. On January 23, 1888, orders arrived transferring them not to
Leavenworth Military Prison but to Alcatraz Island, California.

Completed shortly before Kid's arrival, Alcatraz Prison
boasted 185 wooden cells with two-inch plank flooring covered in sheet iron. The only ventilation in each cell came from
a four-inch gap above the door and a meager two-inch space
below. Fire was always a concern and in March 1888, while Kid
was at Alcatraz, a blaze destroyed several buildings.

The five ex-scouts were freed from Alcatraz in October 1888
after Judge Advocate General G. Norman Lieber successfully
argued the white jury that had convicted them was prejudiced
against the Apaches and the sentences handed down were too
harsh for the crimes committed.

Al Sieber was so angry when the Apache Kid reappeared at
San Carlos he immediately ordered him rearrested. He charged

Kid with attempted murder, claiming his once-trusted scout had fired the bullet that shattered his ankle. Sieber conveniently ignored the fact that Kid had handed over his gun before the shooting started. He also disregarded the time Kid had already served for the San Carlos incident and ordered Gila County Sheriff Glenn Reynolds to lock the former scout in the Globe jail. "That evening," according to Apache Kid biographer Phyllis de la Garza, "bells clanged in the wooden tower of the Methodist church, Globe's customary practice signifying bad Indians were in town."

Sieber swore under oath that Kid had fired the shot that left him crippled for life. On October 30, 1889, the Apache Kid was sentenced to seven years in Yuma Territorial Prison for the attempted murder of his mentor. Two days later he was on his way to Yuma.

Threatening rain clouds hovered overhead that All Saints Day as eight handcuffed Apache convicts shuffled out of the Globe jail and boarded the stagecoach for Yuma Prison. Stage-coach driver Eugene Middleton rubbed the dust off his brand new, heavy-duty, bright green Concord stagecoach with sunny yellow wheels as he watched the men board. Sheriff Reyn-olds and his deputy, William "Hunkydory" Holmes, would escort the prisoners. Kid climbed into the coach and Reynolds secured leg irons on the man considered the most dangerous of his charges.

The stage would carry the prisoners to Casa Grande, a two-day trip from Globe. From there, they would board a train for the final trek into Yuma.

Rain started falling before the stage skidded into the River-side station for the night. After supper the prisoners lined up on benches, their leg irons and handcuffs securely tightened. In this upright position, they tried to sleep.

The next morning the stage had to maneuver the wet and slippery Kelvin Grade, and Middleton feared the coach, laden with passengers, could not make it up the muddy incline. Reynolds ordered the prisoners out of the coach—all except the Apache Kid and the convict shackled to him. Reynolds did not want Kid footloose.

Middleton maneuvered the stage as Reynolds and Holmes escorted the prisoners on foot up Kelvin Grade. The Apaches talked among themselves but since neither Reynolds nor Holmes spoke their language, their conversations were nothing more than gibberish to the two lawmen. Had they understood what the Apaches were saying, it might have saved their lives.

As the stagecoach disappeared around a bend, two prisoners attacked Reynolds while two more grabbed Holmes. Both men died instantly with bullet wounds from their own rifles.

One of the prisoners ran toward the stage and fired at Middleton, sending him tumbling from the coach with a bullet through his mouth and neck. As the prisoners freed Kid and his companion, one angry Indian stood over the paralyzed Middleton ready to smash his head with a rock. For some reason, Kid stopped the man and spared Middleton's life. The Indians disappeared on foot across the desert plains and into the hills they knew so well.

News of the murders spread rapidly. The *Silver Belt* reported bloody clothing was found a few miles from the murder scene. "A carcass of a steer was also discovered, a part of which had been taken and some of the hide stripped off and used for foot-covering, as evidenced by the peculiar tracks made by one of the fugitives after leaving the spot."

Prison photo of Apache Kid taken in 1888 at Globe, Arizona
Courtesy of the Arizona Historical Society/Tucson, AHS #15755

Al Sieber assumed Kid had orchestrated the deadly escape and requested military posses to capture his nemesis. Five Arizona forts responded with troops to track the escapees' trail of destruction.

Although the prisoners were on foot and most were unarmed, the posses were no match for the elusive Apaches. Once, Kid was spotted near the San Carlos River, but he quickly vanished into the hills. Another time, a posse found a cave where the Indians had camped, but they magically disappeared as the law closed in. The fugitives raided ranches and stole horses, then headed farther into the mountains.

Territorial Governor Lewis Wolfley offered a $500 reward for the conviction of any of the outlaw Apaches. Still, no one could catch the swift-footed renegades, who seemed to be making their way toward Mexico.

The Apache Kid and the men who followed him became the most feared Indians in Arizona history. Ranchers were gunned down, their cattle butchered, and horses stolen. Cowboys were found with their heads split open. In March 1890 a freight hauler was murdered near Fort Thomas. That August, three men were killed at Hachita, about fifty miles southwest of Lordsburg, New Mexico. Even western artist Frederick Remington feared crossing Kid's path. While looking for a lost mine in Sonora, Mexico, Remington noted, "The vaqueros I am riding with are not only looking for the lost mine of Tiopa, but are also primed for a fight with the Kid if we cut his trail. And if he cuts ours, we may not live long enough to regret it."

Eventually five of the original eight Apache prisoners were captured; two others killed. By October 1890 only Kid remained free. The *Silver Belt* considered him "a legal target for those who can cock a gun and draw a bead through the sights of a Winchester."

That December, three ranch hands killed an Indian they found butchering one of their steers. From the nearby brush Kid and his men came out shooting. The cowboys took shelter behind a large boulder, and gunfire resounded across the hillside for hours until one of the ranch hands barely dodged a bullet that shattered his corncob pipe. His two buddies, amused at his startled expression, carelessly leaned out from behind their boulder refuge. One was stopped in mid-laugh by a bullet in the head, and it was not long before the second cowboy lay dead. The pipe-smoking gunman headed for the nearest ranch, successfully eluding Kid and his men, but chances are he never lit up a pipe again.

In 1891 an ex-army scout said he chanced upon the Apache Kid in the Santa Catalina Mountains just north of Tucson. Neither man backed off and all day the two sat facing each other, their eyes never leaving the gaze of their adversary, knowing either could kill with one shot. Along about sundown, Kid rose from his rock and announced he was leaving. "As Kid disappeared down the trail, I lit a shuck for home!" the old scout recalled years later.

Occasionally Kid returned to the San Carlos Indian Reservation to retrieve bundles of food, clothing, and ammunition secreted in caves by his family and sympathetic friends. He often took a woman with him when he departed once again for the hills. Some of these women went willingly, others had no choice.

By November 1892 Territorial Governor Nathan Oakes Murphy upped the reward to $6,000 for the capture or death of the Apache Kid. Several Arizona counties offered their own rewards, and since he was blamed for murders in New Mexico Territory as well as south of the border, additional reward money resulted in an accumulated total of $15,000 on his head. Still, no one came near arresting the elusive Indian.

In 1894 Al Sieber, maybe having a change of heart for falsely accusing his trusted scout of attempted murder, tried to get word to Kid that if he would turn himself in, Sieber would help clear his name with the reward money. Sieber waited at several designated spots for Kid to appear, but he never did.

The December 1895 day was bone-chillingly cold as Horatio Merrill and his daughter Eliza steered their wagon from Pima toward the town of Clifton. About six miles from Ash Springs, they were attacked and slain. Lawmen believed at least thirty Indians, led by the Apache Kid, had set upon the pair. When they found the Indians' campsite, they discovered Eliza Merrill's purse. Nestled inside, her newly acquired engagement ring lay undisturbed.

As years passed, tales of the Apache Kid's death began to sprout as often as the offenses laid at his feet. From about 1895 until the mid 1930s, just about everyone had a story to tell. He was found dead in a cave, killed in a cornfield, ambushed at a waterhole, shot off his horse, and slain by Mexican *rurales*.

Arizona pioneer Charles Genung said Kid appeared at his Wickenburg campsite in 1895 obviously dying from consumption. That same year, rancher John Slaughter supposedly followed Kid into Mexico and killed him.

In 1899 the chief of the Mexican *rurales* claimed Kid was living peacefully in the Sierra Madre Mountains.

In 1915 Kid supposedly rode with Pancho Villa, rebel general of the Mexican Revolution.

A nephew of Kid, Joe Adley, said his uncle was still alive in Mexico in 1924. And as late as about 1935, an old cattleman swore he had recently talked with Kid, who claimed he and his family were living in Mexico. After that, the stories stopped.

"Torn between bewildering laws in a white man's world and old Apache tribal traditions, [the Apache Kid] tried adapting to both, and lost," wrote de la Garza. Freedom to live his life according to Apache custom was all Has-kay-bay-nay-ntayl wanted. The price of that freedom cost him dearly.

Wham Paymaster Robbery
The Cattlemen's Caper

In the dim light of dawn, thirteen-year-old Andy Carlson watched wide-eyed as the men tied rags over their horses' mouths to muffle the snorts and whinnies that would surely give them away. For several days the gang had been living in a stifling hot cave surviving on sardines and deviled ham as they erected buttresses above the road that led from Fort Grant to Fort Thomas in southeastern Arizona. This afternoon, the army paymaster would come down this road carrying a payroll close to $30,000. The men had no intention of letting him get to Fort Thomas with his bounty. Young Andy, who would stay behind and hold the horses during the upcoming battle, remembered the events of May 11, 1889, the rest of his life, and he often bragged of his involvement in the greatest military robbery in Arizona history.

Some of the manmade barricades along the ridge were so large that five or six men could hide behind them. Towering sporadic boulders added additional protection. To give the illusion of even more gun power on the hilltop, the men carved yucca stalks to look like rifles, positioning them along the breastworks aimed at the road below. Their final task was to push a huge boulder across the road to block the soldiers' march to Fort Thomas.

At least a dozen men may have been on the hilltop that warm May day, but only seven local cattlemen would be tried for the crime.

Chauncey Gilbert Webb Jr., known as Gilbert, was the likely ringleader of the holdup gang. At age fifty-three he was certainly the oldest participant. He and his sons ran the Webb Cattle Company along with several other businesses near the Mormon community of Pima. Gilbert was a leader in the Church of Jesus Christ of Latter-day Saints, even though an affair with a local widow caused his name to be stricken from church rolls. He fell on hard times during the late 1800s and was forced to sell many of his holdings. At the time of the payroll robbery, he was suspected of illegal cattle branding. At least one of his sons, Wilfred, accompanied his father into the encampment above the road to Fort Thomas.

Mark E. Cunningham also owned a ranch and was eagerly wooing a local gal. He had served as a Graham County deputy sheriff, but lost his bid for sheriff in 1888. His proclivity for gambling may have led to his desire to acquire the army payroll.

Brothers Lyman and Warren Follett, who had a spread nearby, were fingered as part of the robbery gang, along with David Rogers and Thomas Norman Lamb, cowhands on the Webb ranch. All of these men had ties to the Mormon Church except for the gambler, Cunningham.

Mormons had settled the thriving community of Pima along the Gila River in 1879. By the late 1800s, however, ranchers saw their livelihoods shriveling under the desert sun and government taxes. Eastern factions controlled Arizona's purse strings, and the glut of military posts in the territory meant thousands of dollars that could have helped desperate ranchers went into military coffers instead. Discontent was also brewing in religious sectors. Non-Mormons resented the power of the Mormon Church, particularly its influence in local elections. On the other hand, Mormons bristled under the 1882 Edmunds Act that banned plural marriages and gave US marshals authority to arrest those who continued to practice polygamy.

Some or all of these factors may have played a part in the decision of a handful of local cattlemen to seize the army payroll as recompense for the financial, political, and religious hardships they were encountering.

On May 8, 1889, Major Joseph Washington Wham set out from Tucson on his usual pay run. He had been an army paymaster for over ten years, handling innumerable payrolls for the military. He and his retinue stopped first at Fort Huachuca, then continued on to Fort Bowie. They spent the night in Willcox, where Wham picked up more funds waiting at the Willcox railroad depot, money necessary for the payrolls at Forts Grant, Thomas, and Apache, and Camp San Carlos.

A contingent of twelve Buffalo soldiers from the 10th Cavalry and 24th Infantry at Fort Grant relieved Major Wham's initial escort, and he arrived at Fort Grant on May 10 without incident. Wham and his men started for Fort Thomas on Saturday morning, May 11, a run of about forty-five miles. The army ambulance carrying Major Wham led the way while the Buffalo soldiers rode in a second wagon. The heavy oak strongbox in Wham's ambulance, marked U.S. TREASURY, contained $28,345.10 in gold and silver coins.

About fifteen miles from Pima, the two wagons approached a hill descending into Cottonwood Wash, a dry and rocky arroyo. Major Wham's driver led the way, cautiously guiding his team of six mules down the steep hill. The soldiers lightened the load in the second wagon by getting out and walking. Just as the road narrowed, Major Wham's driver pulled to a sharp halt. In front of him, a massive boulder blocked his way.

Chances are it was Wilfred Webb and Mark Cunningham who boldly stood atop the bluff and aimed at the unsuspecting soldiers. As they began firing, Another Follett brother, James Edward, rose up and shot the lead mule attached to the first wagon. Two more mules from the second wagon were dead within seconds. Chaos and bedlam took over the reins as the remaining burros reared and brayed, struggling to get out of harm's way. Caught in a web of tangled harnesses, the mules dragged the wagons, along with their dead companions, off the trail.

From atop the ridge a hailstorm of bullets rained down upon the military entourage. Some say Follett threw a handful of cartridges into a fire behind one of the boulders to give the illusion that hundreds of men were on the rim. The bandits freely scampered from one protective haven to the next, firing down on the small army at will. When one ducked for cover to reload, another popped up, sending a firestorm of lead careening down the hillside. The men seemed to enjoy their game of "cowboys versus cavalry," not even bothering to conceal their identities. One mistake they did make was believing the Buffalo Soldiers would not fight back. The bandits held the white man's belief that black soldiers would panic and run before they would fight.

The soldiers found little protection in the wash and returned fire as they sought refuge behind a low embankment. In less than an hour, Major Wham realized the futility of continuing the skirmish. Although no one was killed, only three soldiers remained unscathed. He ordered his men back beyond the line of fire.

The bandits giddily scurried down from their lofty perch to claim their ill-gotten fortune. They quickly cut the mules' tangled harnesses and chased them away, leaving the wounded soldiers stranded in the middle of the desert. Locating their prize, they hacked open the strongbox, grabbed the treasury bags, and fled.

Laughter rang out as the gunmen scattered. Tracks splayed across the desert with some leading directly toward local ranches, including the Follett ranch.

According to one newspaper report, more than seventeen hundred soldiers and Indian scouts set out in search of the payroll bandits. The trails confused the posses as some of the bandits reversed their horses' shoes, making it appear as if they were riding toward the robbery instead of away. In addition a band of wild horses had recently passed this way, leaving thousands of hoof prints.

The robbery was "without parallel in the history of crime in Arizona," reported the *Arizona Daily Citizen*. "Although seriously encumbered by the weight of money, they [the bandits] are evidently making rapid marches across the mountains, probably trying to get to Mexico."

Because this was a federal crime, US Marshal William Kidder Meade, chief federal law officer in southern Arizona, headed the investigation. Federal agencies, as well as the governor of Arizona, offered numerous rewards for each man caught, enough incentive to round up a slew of suspects.

More than a dozen men were initially arrested and accused of taking part in the robbery. The *St. Johns Herald* protested that all the Mormons in Graham County had been apprehended. After the dust settled and a handful of men were released for lack of evidence (including Ed Follett), seven local cattlemen remained behind bars charged with the robbery of the army payroll.

Public opinion favored the defendants. They were seen as innocent farmers and ranchers who were being persecuted by an overbearing government. Some saw them as "Latter-Day Robin Hoods."

On September 20, 1889, the Arizona Territorial Court for the First Judicial District in Tucson convened. By October 2 they had handed down indictments against all seven defendants for robbing the army payroll. All entered pleas of "not guilty." The trial commenced on November 11.

Over one hundred witnesses were called, more than half testifying for the defense. Everyone had an alibi and a witness to back them up. As the *Arizona Journal-Miner* reported, "If the witnesses for the defense . . . are to be believed, it was a fellow named 'alibi' that robbed the paymaster last May."

The Buffalo soldiers identified several of the defendants as the culprits who fired down from the barricades, but their testimony was tainted by the color of their skin. A black woman, Frankie Campbell, claimed she came upon the cattlemen as they were struggling to move the boulder onto the road. She said she witnessed the entire melee from behind the huge boulder, even sustaining bullet holes in her clothing. She identified most of the bandits by name.

One of the robbers lost a finger in the melee. Lyman Follett showed up in court missing a finger. Gilbert Webb, the only man able to pay his bail and remain free until trial, was accused of bribing witnesses. While out on bail, he paid off some of his debts in gold coins.

The air was filled with accusations and charges, bribery and falsehoods. Judges and lawyers came and went as each side accused the other of collusion and deceit.

Reenactment photo taken the day after the Wham Paymaster robbery
Courtesy of the Arizona Historical Society/Tucson, AHS #44754

On December 10, 1889, it was all over. The jurors were handed the case on December 14, and within two hours, including a lunch break, the jury of twelve free white men returned to the courtroom and acquitted the seven cattlemen of any wrongdoing. No one was ever convicted of robbing the army payroll.

Little changed in the tiny hamlet of Pima, Arizona Territory. Gilbert Webb lost his home over unpaid taxes, but he was eventually reinstated into the Mormon Church and served as a delegate to the Territorial Democratic Convention in 1890. Wilfred Webb, or W. T. as he was now called, entered politics serving as speaker of the Arizona House of Representatives and member of the Arizona Constitutional Convention. His spread, the 76 Ranch, was eventually turned into a dude ranch.

Andy Carlson, the wide-eyed teenager who held the horses' reins as the robbery unfolded, remained a cowboy all his life.

The other acquitted men fell in and out with the law, but none ever admitted any part in the Wham payroll robbery.

Speculation still abounds whether the bulk of the army money may be stashed somewhere near the town of Pima, but in all probability it is long gone.

Of the dozen Buffalo soldiers who defended the army payroll, two were awarded the Medal of Honor and eight received commendations from the military.

Major Wham, initially charged with replacing the funds lost on his watch, eventually was released from his financial burden by Congress.

In his later years, W. T. Webb was often asked if he had any part in the heist. His reply never wavered: "I neither confirm nor deny any involvement. To confirm would be to admit my guilt, but to deny would surely ruin a good story."

Augustine Chacón
Hombre Muy Malo

On the evening of December 18, 1895, Paul Becker, a clerk tending Mrs. McCormack's store in southern Arizona's Morenci Canyon, locked up and headed for the local saloon to grab a bite to eat. Three men watched him leave. Augustine Chacón, Pilar Franco, and Leonardo Morales climbed through a transom at the rear of the store looking for money, guns, food—anything they could steal.

After Becker had his fill at the saloon, he headed back to McCormack's and walked in on the bandits. They ordered him to open the store safe. Becker lunged at the trio, knocking the gun out of one man's hand and grabbing for a knife held by another. The knife sliced across Becker's hand. They again demanded he open the safe and again Becker refused. According to Becker's later statement, Augustine Chacón then plunged a knife into the clerk's side and left him for dead. The three men departed the way they came, richer by a mere twenty-five dollars and two watches. Becker staggered back to the saloon where Constable Alex Davis removed the six-inch knife still stuck in his side.

Augustine Chacón, a man who admitted to killing over fifty men during his lifetime, had struck fear around Morenci and across most of southern Arizona, long before he entered McCormack's store that night. And while his life did not start out on the wrong side of the law, he ended up on the wrong end of a hangman's noose.

Born in Sonora, Mexico, around 1856, Chacón claimed he worked as a farmhand and *vaquero* (cowboy), even hiring on for a while with the Mexican border patrol. Around 1888 he arrived in Morenci and was employed as a cowboy on Ben Ollney's ranch. Over six feet tall with a mass of black hair covering his body, including a voluminous beard and mustache, he aptly fit his nickname *El Peludo* or "The Hairy One."

Chacón earned the respect of his *compadres* on the ranch and his boss found no fault with his work until the day Chacón disputed the size of his paycheck. Chacón and Ollney exchanged heated words, and at one point Ollney purportedly laughed in Chacón's face. Ollney drew his gun but was no match for the wily cowboy. When the smoke cleared, the rancher lay dying in the dust. Ranch hands raced to his rescue, but five cowboys also met their fate at the end of Chacón's gun.

Chacón hightailed it into the hills with a posse in hot pursuit. They quickly caught up with him but Chacón knew if he could not outrun a posse, he could certainly outshoot them. He killed four before a bullet smacked into his arm, yet he still managed to escape.

Chacón eluded the law for several months until someone recognized him one night near Fort Apache. Although he argued his innocence, a vigilante group threw him in jail with the promise of a sunrise hanging.

When the first streaks of dawn peered between the barred windows of Chacón's cell, only a pile of hacksaw blades and a few sawed-off bars lay where the outlaw should have been sleeping. Some said Nelly Ollney, the rancher's daughter, who never believed Chacón murdered her father, provided the tools for his escape.

For the next few years, Chacón roamed back and forth across the Mexican border, earning his living by smuggling cattle and horses from one country to the other. He was back in Morenci by early 1894.

One cold winter morning, two clerks who worked at the nearby Detroit Copper Company made camp at Eagle Creek to enjoy a few days of hunting and fishing. When a band of outlaws came upon them, the naïve young men stood no chance. The bandits were after guns and ammunition and lost little time eliminating the campers to acquire their goods. No one witnessed the killings, but Chacón was the name Morenci citizens put to the merciless slayings.

For a while Chacón hung around the town of Tombstone where outlaws and lawmen were often one and the same. It was not long before Cochise County Sheriff John Slaughter caught wind of Chacón's presence. Determined to bring him in, Slaughter and his deputy, Burt Alvord, found their man visiting friends in a large tent just outside of town. Alvord covered the front of the canvas building, Slaughter the back.

As Chacón fled out the back way, Slaughter fired, certain he had hit his man even though the night was as black as *El Peludo*'s heart. Slaughter noticed one of the tent's guy ropes had broken and assumed Chacón had tripped over it, dying as he rolled down a ravine running behind the tent.

With lanterns lighting the way, the lawmen headed down the abyss. But the ditch gave up no body. Chacón had apparently tethered his horse below for a quick getaway. Unscathed, he probably tripped over the rope just as Slaughter fired.

Augustine Chacón, "The Hairy One"
Courtesy of the Arizona Historical Society/Tucson, AHS #PC 161/F.5/I

By now Chacón had few places he felt safe, but for some reason he kept returning to Morenci. Then came the break-in at McCormack's store.

The day after the robbery, Constable Davis, who was also a Graham County deputy sheriff, gathered a posse and followed the bandits' trail up a steep hill to a lowly cabin. From inside Chacón watched the posse approach. Suddenly, he bolted out the door, quickly followed by Franco and Morales. Gunfire exploded across the hillside as the bandits took refuge behind a barrier of huge boulders.

Eventually, Franco and Morales got to their horses and headed down the hill. Several of the posse followed, killing both men as they fled.

The war continued at the cabin. One member of the posse, Pablo Salcido, was a friend of Chacón's from their days as cowboys. Salcido convinced Davis he could talk the bandit into surrendering. He called to Chacón, and Chacón invited him to come ahead. As Salcido advanced, Chacón stepped into the open and fired one shot, felling his friend with a bullet through the head.

A hail of gunfire rained down upon the killer. Spent shells outnumbered the scraggly wildflowers scattered across the barren hillside in the bloodiest gunfight in Morenci history.

Suddenly an eerie silence greeted the posse. Cautiously, they approached the boulder and found Chacón dazed with a bullet in his shoulder and a streak across his chest where another bullet had grazed him. Once again, *El Peludo* would be behind bars. But for how long?

Chacón recuperated in the tiny Solomonville jail, a facility the *Arizona Republican* ridiculed as "the most insecure in the Territory." Charged with the murder of Pablo Salcido, he wasted no time proving the newspaper article correct when he casually walked out of his cell one evening. Crouching in a nearby ditch, he waited for a chance to flee out of town. His freedom was short-lived when one of the men looking for him tripped and fell into the ditch on top of him.

On May 26, 1896, Chacón appeared before the Solomon-ville court and pled innocent to the killing of Pablo Salcido, claiming he would never shoot his friend. Despite his plea, he was convicted of murder and the hanging set for July 24, 1896. To ensure he would still be around, he was sent to a more secure jail in Tucson until the date of his execution.

Although Chacón appealed his case to the Supreme Court of Arizona Territory, the initial verdict was upheld. A group of citizens opposing the death penalty petitioned he serve life in the Yuma Territorial Prison, but they were also turned down. One newspaper claimed there was "a sentiment in Graham County amounting almost to a religious fervour [*sic*] against hanging [Chacón]." The delays extended his execution date to June 18, 1897. As he was being escorted back to Solomonville, he managed to saw off his shackles. This escape attempt was quickly thwarted.

With only nine days to go before he faced the gallows, Chacón seemed destined, finally, to die. But The Hairy One had other ideas.

No one knew where he acquired his supply of tools. Visiting friends probably brought them in piece by piece. A band of sympathetic Mexican prisoners supposedly played guitars and sang a selection of loud, lively songs as he cut his shackles, burrowed into the thick adobe wall of his cell, and sawed through broad beams embedded in the stone walls. When he finally broke through, he tumbled into the sheriff's office and sailed out the window, once again a free man.

For the next five years, Chacón hid out on both sides of the border. More than one unsolved crime was blamed on him, and he probably did commit his share, such as the 1899 murders of two men found in their home near New River, their house ransacked and robbed by a group of marauders. The posse that trailed the culprits through Pinal County into Globe, then along the Black River, garnered a description of the men from ranchers they passed. One of the desperadoes certainly fit Chacón's hairy countenance, but the killers were never caught.

In the late 1800s as the country expanded westward and territories attained statehood, Arizona Territory was repeatedly rejected in its bid for sovereignty. A major detriment facing Arizona was its reputation as a place where outlaws could still find refuge. In 1901 Territorial Governor Nathan Oakes Murphy organized the Arizona Rangers to enforce territorial law. Range boss Burton C. Mossman became the first captain of this new breed of lawmen; and during his one-year term, he and his men eliminated some of the most notorious outlaw gangs in the territory. Mossman was determined to bring in Augustine Chacón before his term was up. By now Chacón only came into Arizona when he needed to sell off rustled Mexican cattle or horses.

In April 1902 Mossman recruited two lawmen-turned-outlaws to help him capture Chacón—ex-deputy constable Billy Stiles and Burt Alvord, the man who had once tried to capture Chacón with Sheriff Slaughter. Mossman promised leniency for the two scoundrels if they helped with his plot. They were to contact Chacón at his Mexican hideout and entice him to cross the border into Arizona. Since Arizona Rangers had no authority in Mexico, he needed to get Chacón into the United States before he could arrest him. Mossman posed as an escaped horse thief who desired some of rancher Colonel Bill Green's fine racehorses located just this side of the US-Mexico border, and he wanted Chacón to sell the herd in Mexico. After sending the two reprobates into Mexico to contact Chacón, Mossman waited to see if the killer would take the bait. It was four months before he heard from his accomplices.

On August 31 Stiles met Mossman in the border town of Naco and handed the ranger a note from Alvord saying Chacón agreed to a meeting, "twenty-five miles within the Mexican line at the Socorro Mountain spring . . ."

Mossman was not eager to cross into Mexico, well aware that if a Mexican patrol caught him arresting one of its citizens within its borders, he would be in deep trouble. But he was determined to get his man, so he and Stiles headed south. Three days later they met up with Chacón and Alvord.

Chacón was a reluctant host. His eyes never left the stranger who promised him good horseflesh. As Mossman, Alvord, and Stiles drank whiskey and exchanged small talk during the night, Chacón remained sober and silent. A drizzling rain left the men cold and uncomfortable, although Mossman had the protection of his yellow rain slicker. Beneath it, his hand never left the hilt of his gun.

The next morning Mossman warmed himself by the fire. He pulled out a smoldering twig, bowed his head against the morning breeze, and breathed deeply to ignite his tightly rolled cigarette. He glanced over at Chacón, and there was no question in Mossman's mind who was in charge around this campfire.

He willed himself to make no suspect moves that would anger his smoking partner. He had one chance to get the drop on Chacón. If he faltered, he would be dead before his cigarette hit the ground.

Alvord saddled his horse saying he would bring back fresh water. He had no intention of returning.

Wiping his brow, Mossman realized it was not the morning rain drizzling down his face but his own sweat. He knew he had to act now.

In one swift motion, he dropped the burning twig into the fire, reached beneath his slicker, drew out his gun, and arrested one of the most notorious murderers in southern Arizona. The fact that the capture was illegal made no difference to Mossman at the moment. He ordered Stiles to disarm Chacón and handcuff him.

The three men rode out of camp with Stiles in the lead, holding the reins of Chacón's horse. Chacón traveled with a rope around his neck and his hands cuffed behind his back. Mossman brought up the rear as the outlaw parade made its way back into US territory. Mossman watched his back for any signs of a Mexican patrol. His one-year commission as an Arizona Ranger had just expired.

Once in the United States, Mossman flagged down a train heading into Benson for the final leg of the trip. Graham County Sheriff Jim Parks met the entourage with a new pair of handcuffs for Chacón and a set of leg irons.

A reporter on the train noted the haggard face of the forty-six-year-old bandit. "His form is bent and his beard is tinged with gray. To be hunted like a wild animal for five years has left its mark on the outlaw . . ." When asked where he was going, Chacón remarked, "I suppose they are taking me to

Solomonville, and I want them to kill me this time. I prefer death to a term in the penitentiary."

When the reporter asked Mossman where he had captured Chacón, Mossman replied, ". . . on a horse pasture located about seven miles this side of the Mexican line." Mossman and Sheriff Parks must have had a few moments to get their story straight because Parks backed up the lie.

Guards were posted outside the Solomonville jail, which had undergone a few changes since Chacón's last visit, including a new steel cage made just for him. However, the same gallows built in 1897 still waited, ensconced behind a fourteen-foot adobe wall to keep out the curious. Only those with invitations would be allowed to view the hanging.

The execution was scheduled for November 14, 1902, but once again, a citizens group petitioned to commute the sentence to life imprisonment, and once again, the argument was defeated. The date of the hanging was changed to November 21—Black Friday.

Chacón ate a hearty breakfast the morning of his execution, then visited with friends Sixto Molina and Jesus Bustos. He talked to the local Catholic priest several times during the day and finished off a big lunch. He put on a new black suit and shaved off his scraggly beard, leaving his drooping mustache intact. At 2:00 p.m. he headed toward the gallows.

As he entered the courtyard, about fifty people greeted him. Even more climbed nearby trees for a glimpse of *El Peludo*. He made his way up the steps of the gallows, passing the coffin that awaited him.

Chacón asked if he could have a cup of coffee and a cigarette before dying. He turned to the crowd and spoke to them in

Spanish with an interpreter repeating his words. "It is nothing but right that when one is going to die that he be given a few moments of time to quietly smoke a cigarette," he said.

For thirty minutes he rambled on, once again swearing his innocence in the shooting of Pablo Salcido. "I have a clean conscience," he said. Raising his hand, he swore, "I am sure that this hand has never been guilty of murder. I may have stolen and done a good many other things, but I am innocent of this crime."

He asked for another cup of coffee, then sat down on the gallows steps to roll another cigarette and continue his conversation with the crowd. Finally, he was silent. "Is that all?" asked the interpreter. "Si, es todo (Yes, that's all)," Chacón replied.

Friends climbed the gallows steps to shake his hand. He asked to be allowed to live until 3:00 p.m., but his request was denied. "It's too late now," he said. "Time to hang." He was pronounced dead sixteen minutes later. Molina and Bustos carted off the body of their friend and buried him a few miles from Solomonville in San Jose.

The Arizona Bulletin reported the next day, "A nervier man than Augustine Chacón never walked to the gallows, and his hanging was a melodramatic spectacle that will never be forgotten by those who witnessed it."

Many years after Chacón's hanging, historian Ryder Ridgeway claimed he was giving a speech on outlaws in Oakland, California, when he noticed a stoic-looking man in the front row. The stranger showed little emotion as Ridgeway talked until he mentioned the name Augustine Chacón. Suddenly the man was consumed with grief, tears streaming down his face. As Ridgeway concluded his speech, the man approached and bombarded him with questions about Chacón. Ridgeway asked what interest the stranger had in the old outlaw, and the man said he was Chacón's son. His mother had kept the facts of his father's reputation from him, saying he had died in Solomonville during a smallpox epidemic. Now he knew the truth.

In 1980 some of Chacón's family members dedicated a marble gravestone to the outlaw in the San Jose cemetery. On the marker, they inscribed the following words:

AUGUSTINE CHACÓN
1861 — 1902
he lived life without fear,
he faced death without fear.
HOMBRE MUY BRAVO

Maybe he was *muy bravo* to some, but to most he was the *hombre muy malo* (very bad man).

James Fleming Parker
"I Died Game and like a Man"

In the dwindling twilight, James Fleming Parker stumbled along the snow-slick trail of Diamond Creek Canyon near the foot of the majestic Grand Canyon. The chasm held nothing but a deep abyss from which he would never return if his foot slipped on the treacherous path. The small caves that dotted the sheer walls held other terrors. Mountain lions and black bears made their homes along these steep parapets, and Parker certainly did not want to spoil their sleep as he balanced gingerly on the precipice.

But what lay behind him was even more worrisome. A posse had been on his trail for days; he was exhausted and hungry. Traveling by foot since no horse could keep its footing on the rugged prominences, he had even walked through ice-encrusted waters to elude the persistent lawmen. As he crawled beneath a sheltering boulder, he dared not light a fire to warm his shivering, starving body. He found a flat stone and laid his head on the makeshift pillow. Parker knew he had made this cold, hard bed himself, and now he had to lie in it.

That snowy night in February 1897 was not the first time Parker had run afoul of the law. From his first breath in 1865, he was doomed to a life of hardship and trouble. At the age of fifteen, after his mother had died in childbirth and his father committed suicide, he was sentenced to California's San Quentin Penitentiary for stealing a steer.

Upon his release the teenager drifted into Arizona Territory and worked as a cowboy in the Prescott area. He became close friends with another ranch hand, George Ruffner, who would figure prominently in Parker's life, and death.

Parker was an excellent wrangler. He and Ruffner participated in the July 4, 1888, Prescott rodeo, an event the town claims to be the first rodeo in history.

Parker never stayed in one place long. He returned to California and once again landed in San Quentin for stealing a farmer's wheat supply. Originally sentenced to five years, he was released on a technicality after serving only nine months.

By 1895 he was back in Arizona working for Charlie "Hog-Eye" Miller at the Hat Ranch near Williams, Arizona, a town made up of lean-to shacks, one church, and about thirty saloons.

Parker had been at the Hat Ranch just a few months when horses and cattle began disappearing around northern Arizona at an alarming rate. A breeder who hired Parker to break a band of wild horses soon discovered several of his herd missing, but he did not initially suspect the good-looking, personable young man. However, after Parker started hanging out with Abe Thompson and his gang, known cattle and horse rustlers, the breeder suspected his hired hand of instigating the theft.

Abe Thompson and his men roamed northern Arizona pilfering cattle and horses, then driving them to market in southern Nevada. When more than forty horses turned up missing from a loading pen near Seligman, Thompson's gang was immediately suspected of the heist. Although a posse caught two of the rustlers, the rest of the gang escaped, riding into their almost unapproachable hideout in Robber's Roost, a canyon surrounded by towering walls and treacherous trails that lay near the confluence of Diamond Creek with the Colorado River.

Parker continued to remain relatively free of the law even though his name was often associated with missing livestock. In 1896 he went to work for Tom Wagner on the Bar Cross Ranch, near Williams, and had an opportunity to show his more compassionate side when Wagner got caught between a calf he had roped to brand and its irate mother. As the bovine took off after him and with only one direction to run, Wagner was heading straight toward a cliff when Parker rode up and lassoed the cow, saving Wagner from certain death.

Parker eventually became the undisputed leader of the Thompson gang. He preferred rustling horses over cattle, as they were easier to move about and did not complain as loudly. Yet he was looking for even more excitement and much more money.

Trains had been running through Prescott since 1887 carrying gold bullion out of California to wealthy eastern investors. Parker had no love of locomotion, particularly after a train hit two of his own horses and he received a mere pittance from the railroad for his loss. He decided to hit up one of the trains to get his fair settlement. He was not at all concerned about an 1888 law that made train robbery a capital offense punishable by hanging.

He set about determining when gold was scheduled to be shipped through Arizona on the Atlantic & Pacific Railroad and soon learned a healthy amount of bullion would be transported on the eastbound train February 8, 1897. The train would have to slow almost to a crawl as it struggled up a steep grade and maneuvered a sharp curve at Rock Cut, about halfway between Peach Springs and Nelson, small whistle stops along Arizona's northern frontier.

Parker rode into Peach Springs, sold his horse, and bought a one-way ticket to Barstow, telling everyone he had obtained work in California. When he climbed aboard the westbound train, he carried only his saddle, a bedroll, and his guns.

As the train pulled into Barstow, Parker got off, turned around, and boarded an eastbound commuter for southern Nevada. From there he acquired a horse and made his way back into Arizona. He took only one accomplice with him as he headed for Rock Cut, a man named Williams or Wilson whose true identity was never known.

On the night of February 8, the two men tethered their horses behind a small thicket along the tracks, the fire from copious cigarettes their only warmth. As the train slowed at the curve, Parker grabbed the ladder, jumped aboard the locomotive, leveled his gun on the engineer and fireman, and ordered them to stop the train. His partner was to uncouple the engine and express car, then fire two shots alerting Parker to move the two cars away from the rest of the train. They would unload the gold from the express car and be on their way. When Parker heard the signal, he commanded the engineer to move the locomotive and second car a few miles down the tracks.

He tied up the engineer and fireman and climbed into what he thought was the express car. On this train, however, the mail car had been coupled to the locomotive instead of the expected express car loaded with gold. Parker made the best of the situation and rifled through the mail looking for anything of value. He got away with about $5.

When the train made its unexpected stop, both the Wells Fargo agent and mail clerk knew something was up. With guns drawn, they cautiously made their way to the front of the train where they spotted the second outlaw uncoupling the cars. The two shots Parker heard were those that killed his accomplice.

After his colleague failed to appear, Parker untied the engineer and fireman and instructed them to take the locomotive back down the track, couple the cars together, and get out of there. He watched as the train passed by and stayed nearby until morning. At dawn's light, the only sign of his partner was blood on the tracks. Parker took off for Robber's Roost.

When the robbery was reported in Peach Springs, George Ruffner, who was now the Yavapai County sheriff, along with Coconino County Sheriff Ralph Cameron and Mohave County Sheriff Bill Lake, plus a handful of deputies and Indian trackers, took up the search for the lone train robber.

For days the posse stayed close on Parker's trail, even following the circles he rode in to confuse them. Eventually the path became more rigorous and the temperature soon dropped below freezing. When fresh snow eliminated all traces of Parker's whereabouts, the posse finally quit. Parker watched the men ride out of the canyon toward town.

The outlaw was also suffering from the elements, however. To keep his feet from freezing, he walked rather than rode his horse. At some point he removed his boots and wrapped clothing around his feet, maybe after fording Diamond Creek. He slept in caves with a rock for his pillow. Yet as cold as he was, he believed he had escaped unscathed.

On February 22, back on the trail with fresh horses, the posse camped in a side canyon that emptied into Diamond Creek. A couple of deputies scouring for firewood came upon a tethered horse, its hoof prints matching those they had been following. One of the men stayed behind while the other reported back to camp. Soon a whistling Parker came strolling up the creek bed, his Winchester rifle casually draped across his shoulder. The deputy wasted no time making his presence, and his gun, known to the train robber. The outlaw gave up without incident.

Parker was incarcerated in Prescott and charged with train robbery. He shared a cell with accused forger Lewis C. Miller and Cornelia Sarata (sometimes spelled Asarta), arrested for assault. As always, Parker soon tired of his surroundings and desired a new location. On May 9, 1897, he escaped along with Miller and Sarata. If he had stayed in jail, he might have received a fairly light sentence since his bounty from the train robbery was so small. But when he made his bid for freedom, things did not go well.

The warm spring day afforded no breeze through the stifling jail. The prisoners demanded water. Jailer Robert Meador allowed Sarata, a trustee, to fetch a couple of buckets to quench their thirsts. Returning with full water buckets, Sarata stood behind Meador as the jailer unlocked the cell door. Parker rammed the door into Meador's face. Sarata wrestled him to the ground as Parker grabbed the heavy ring of jail keys and slugged Meador over the head.

Parker ran into the next room and grabbed a handful of weapons. He was almost to the front door when Assistant County Attorney Lee Norris, hearing Meador's cries, dashed down the stairs to see what the ruckus was about. As soon as he saw Parker, Norris turned in retreat, but Parker had no intention of letting the attorney sound an alarm. The bullet hit Norris square in the back. He lingered through the night but died before dawn. Norris had just asked his sweetheart to marry him.

Parker, Sarata, and Miller raced to a livery stable across from the jail. Parker was a connoisseur of good horseflesh, having once asserted, "They'll hang you just as high for stealin' a sorry hoss as for the best." He needed only an instant to spot the finest horse in the stable, a pure white beauty considered the fastest steed in the territory. Sure-Shot belonged to his old pal Sheriff Ruffner. Parker jumped aboard Sure-Shot while Miller and Sarata grabbed another horse and rode double as the trio hightailed it out of town.

About 150 men set out after the escaped prisoners. Ruffner, who was out of town when the jailbreak occurred, caught up with the posse at Lynx Creek where they had cornered the three desperadoes. Shots rang out as the two sides squared off. Miller suddenly fell from the horse he shared with Sarata. Parker plucked Miller from the ground and onto Sure-Shot as he fled from the battle.

Some sources claim Jailer Meador fired three shots as the men fled their cells, one bullet hitting Sarata. Others believe Sarata was wounded at Lynx Creek. Whatever shape he was in, as Miller climbed aboard Sure-Shot, Sarata rode off, never to be seen again.

Parker and Miller raced across the valley with the posse and a team of bloodhounds in hot pursuit. Eventually, the two men parted ways with Miller heading toward Jerome on foot and nursing a wound he received either at the hands of Jailer Meador or at the Lynx Creek skirmish. Nine days later, he gave himself up. Parker, however, was in no mood to return to the Prescott jail.

"Parker, the train robber and murderer, with a pack of bloodhounds and officers of the law on his trail, has baffled his pursuers and no doubt is safe from pursuit in the wilds of a country no one is more familiar with than he," bemoaned one May 16 newspaper article. ". . . the fox is smarter than the hounds."

Look Out for

Train Robber and Murderer.

$1000 REWARD

For the Arrest and Conviction of

FLEMING PARKER

Who escaped from County Jail at Prescott, Arizona, on or about May 13, 1897. In making his escape he shot and mortally wounded the Deputy District Attorney.

DESCRIPTION.

Fleming Parker, alias William Parker, is now about 31 years of age; 5 feet 7½ inches high; weighs 165 lbs.; light grey eyes; brown hair; size of foot 6½ inches; teeth in fair condition; high, full forehead; round features; straight nose; small mouth; round chin; vacine mark on left forearm; mole back of neck; scar on left side of head. Usually wears his hat on back of his head; is a cowboy by occupation, and a native of Tulare County. His picture as given hereon is a perfect likeness of him. He has served a term of five years in San Quentin for burglary. When last heard of he was heading for Nevada or Utah; had a repeating rifle with him. He was arrested for attempting to rob the A. & P. R. R. train at Peach Springs, Arizona, and was being held for trial in the Prescott Jail when he escaped. His partner Jim, alias Harry Williams of Utah, was killed at the time of the attempted robbery. There is no doubt of his conviction if captured. If arrested telegraph Sheriff Ruffner, Prescott, Arizona, or the undersigned.

J. N. THACKER,

SPECIAL OFFICER, WELLS, FARGO & CO.,

SAN FRANCISCO

SAN FRANCISCO, May 18, 1897.

Wanted poster distributed by Wells Fargo & Co. for capture of Parker
Courtesy of the Sharlot Hall Museum Library and Archives, Prescott, Arizona, #104PE

Parker made good time heading back to Robber's Roost, his old haunt. But Sheriff Ruffner was determined not to let the murderer and horse thief get away, particularly on his prize mount. He put up $1,000 of his own money for Parker's capture, bringing the total on the outlaw's head to $4,000. The two men, who knew each other so well from their days as cowboys, stayed almost within shooting distance of each other, but Parker knew the terrain better and continually eluded his adversary.

He even had time for a little tomfoolery. Ruffner came across a piece of paper Parker had placed conspicuously on the trail. "A reward of $1,000 is offered by the undersigned for Sheriff Ruffner dead or alive," the note read, "—dead preferred."

Parker hid out with a band of sheepmen who obliterated his tracks by herding their flock across his path. The sheepmen had no use for lawmen who often gave them trouble.

As he made his way toward Robber's Roost, Parker happened upon an empty ranch house. He took time to reshod Sure-Shot, putting the horse's shoes on backwards and riding along the river bottom for several miles to confuse the posse before properly replacing the horse's shoes.

Tom Wagner, the man who owed his life to Parker, found one of his best horses missing one day. In its place stood a very tuckered-out Sure-Shot. With his proclivity for good horseflesh, Parker soon abandoned Wagner's horse and acquired another from a livery stable in Williams.

Parker's trail eventually led to Hog-Eye Miller's Ranch, a place he was still welcome. When the bloodhounds picked up his scent, he headed into the Bill Williams Mountains, a tough ride for any man, horse, or dog over jagged granite rocks and loose shale. As the posse followed, the hounds' paws were soon torn and bleeding as they scrambled through the rough terrain, forcing the posse to return to town.

The next morning, sporting booties on their feet, the dogs picked up the scent again, but within a short time they began sneezing and howling. Parker had sprinkled pepper along the trail.

On May 23 two Navajos spotted Parker camping near the Little Colorado River and reported their discovery to Samuel S. Preston, proprietor of a local trading post. Preston notified Sheriff Cameron in Flagstaff who immediately telegraphed Sheriff Ruffner in Prescott.

Not waiting for Ruffner to join them, Preston, Cameron, and about ten Navajo trackers headed out to find their prey. Just before daylight on May 26, the posse crept into Parker's camp as his fire smoldered and his horse snorted nervously in the predawn air. When one of the Indians fired a shot, Parker awoke with a start, a dozen guns aimed at his head.

With the outlaw in tow, the men started for Flagstaff, camping for the night near the Little Colorado River. Never one to give up when the odds looked decidedly against him, Parker strategized he would grab one of the tracker's guns and escape into the surrounding heavy brush. He was just about to make his move when Ruffner rode into camp to join the posse. Parker knew he stood no chance of eluding his old buddy.

He was placed in the Flagstaff jail where Lewis Miller was already occupying a cell. Not willing to take his eyes off his nemesis, Ruffner spent the night on a cot outside Parker's cell.

The next morning, with shackles on their feet, Parker and Miller hobbled their way to the train station for the ride into Prescott.

Just outside the tiny town of Whipple, the train made an unscheduled stop and Ruffner hustled the two outlaws off the train and into a waiting wagon. He had been warned that a lynch mob was forming at the Prescott depot so he ordered his prisoners be taken directly to the courthouse, determined they would arrive with their heads intact.

Ruffner's information was not quite accurate. About two hundred men were waiting in Prescott, but they were at the courthouse, not the train station. When Ruffner pulled up, Miller panicked. "My God, they're coming to hang us," he cried. Parker was more philosophical. "Try to have a little courage," he told Miller. "They can only hang you once." Ruffner, with his twin-barreled shotgun loaded and aimed, stoically told the crowd to go home.

On June 15, 1897, Parker was tried for the murder of Lee Norris. It took only three days to find him guilty. He was never charged with the train robbery.

Miller was given a life sentence as an accessory in Norris's murder. He served ten years in Yuma Territorial Prison and was released.

Parker's hanging was scheduled for Friday, August 13, but legal delays and appeals postponed the execution until June 3, 1898.

Supposedly acquiring religion while awaiting his fate, Parker was baptized into the Catholic faith just days before his hanging. On the eve of his last day on earth, however, when Ruffner asked if he had any last requests, the condemned man purportedly requested a visit from Flossie, one of the girls on Whiskey Row.

The morning of the hanging, Ruffner read Parker the death warrant and escorted him to the scaffold. Given the chance to speak, Parker replied, "I claim that I am getting something that ain't due me, but I guess every man who is about to be hanged says the same thing, so that don't cut no figure; whenever the people says I must go, I am one who can go and make no kick."

As the black hood was placed over his head, he asked it be removed so he could shake hands with everyone on the scaffold. When he got to the jailer, he gave him a message for the other prisoners. "[T]ell the boys that I died game and like a man," he said.

He requested his old friend, George Ruffner, replace the hood. As he did so, Ruffner sprang the trap that sent Parker to his death.

James Fleming Parker was taken to potter's field for burial. Sheriff George Ruffner drove the hearse.

Pearl Hart

Pearl of the West

Henry Bacon whistled to keep himself company as he drove the stagecoach along the Globe road toward Florence, a distance of about sixty miles.

> *The sun was brightly shining on a pleasant afternoon*
> *My partner speaking lightly said, "The stage will be here soon."*
> *We saw it coming around the bend and called to them to halt,*
> *And to their pockets we attended, if they got hurt it was their fault.*

The May breeze blew warmly across his face and brought back memories of days when he was one of many stagecoach drivers traveling across the stark Arizona desert. Now, he chauffeured one of the last stage routes in existence, and there was none of the old excitement in the journey.

He missed the camaraderie of a sidekick shotgun rider who watched for dastardly robbers waiting in ambush. Stagecoaches used to carry gold-laden strongboxes and packages of registered mail filled with lucrative stashes of cash and jewelry. With the expansion of railroads across the nation, most gold shipments these days traveled by train, and he could not remember the last time he had heard of a stagecoach robbery.

His three passengers nodded off as the afternoon sun permeated the coach. Slowing to maneuver the curve near Cane Springs Canyon, Bacon spotted a couple of cowboys hailing him to stop. *Probably need a lift,* he thought. *Might as well pick 'em up. Got plenty of room and no strongbox on board.*

As he reined in the horses, the two strangers suddenly pulled pistols and aimed directly at Bacon. They ordered his hands up and relieved him of his Colt .45 revolver, then pulled the passengers out of the coach.

They were an odd pair, Bacon thought as he steadied the horses. The one leveling a gun at his chest sported a shock of dark hair dangling from a scrunched-down hat and looked to be in his mid-twenties. And while this man seemed perfectly capable of shooting anyone who disagreed with him, it was the other bandit that caught Bacon's attention.

The second robber was particularly small, and at first Bacon thought he might be a young boy, maybe about fifteen years old. But as he looked closer, he realized that the soft gray eyes peering from beneath the oversized white sombrero and the easily identifiable bosom underneath the gray flannel shirt belonged to a woman. As she blistered off a litany of cussedness, she rifled through the passengers' pockets and came up with around $400.

> While the birds were sweetly swinging, and the men stood up in line
> And the silver softly ringing as it touched this palm of mine.
> There we took their money, but left them enough to eat
> And the men looked so funny as they vaulted to their seats.

The lady bandit searched inside the coach and retrieved two guns. ". . . I can't see why men carry revolvers," she would later muse, "because they almost invariably give them up at the very time they were made to be used."

Bacon also carried a few dollars, and the two robbers let him keep his money, but the woman tucked the driver's revolver into her waistband. The bandits gallantly returned $1 to each passenger to pay for grub when they arrived in town.

After ordering the passengers back into the coach, the outlaws turned and fled into the hills.

Then up the road we galloped, quickly through a canyon we did pass
Over the mountains we went swiftly, trying to find our horses grass,
Past the station we boldly went, now along the riverside,
And our horses being spent, of course we had to hide.

Bacon whipped his horses into a frenzy and hightailed it back to Globe to report the robbery. As soon as Pinal County Sheriff William E. Truman was notified, he formed a posse and set out after the culprits. Truman was pretty sure he knew the outlaws. Joe Boot, a downtrodden miner and jack-of-all-trades, had been seen in the area recently with Pearl Hart, a woman of questionable character.

The chase lasted just a few days, as the two bandits left a trail even a tenderfoot could follow. With no apparent plan of escape, Boot and Pearl drifted through the towns of Riverside and Mammoth. They slept during the day and traveled at night, stole food for themselves and hay for their horses, and got thoroughly drenched when torrential rains hit the area. One day, they crawled into a cave for shelter and met up with an angry musk hog, which Boot shot.

In the night we would travel, in the daytime try and rest,
And throw ourselves on the gravel, to sleep we would try our best.
Around us our horses were stamping, looking for some hay or grain,
On the road the Posse was tramping, looking for us all in vain.

Four days after the daring daylight robbery, Sheriff Truman walked up to the pair sleeping on the rain-soaked ground, grabbed their weapons, nudged them awake with the toe of his boot, and arrested them for robbing the stagecoach. Boot placidly surrendered, but Pearl let out a torrent of expletives damning first the sheriff and then Boot for not putting up a fight. Truman was grateful the lady wildcat could not reach her gun. "She would have killed me in my tracks could she had got to her pistol," he said a few days later. "Surely women are curious creatures."

> One more day they would not have got us, but my horse got sore and thin,
> And my partner was a mean cuss, so Billy Truman roped us in.
> Thirty years my partner got, I was given five,
> He seemed contented with his lot, and I am still alive.

According to the *Arizona Sentinel*, Pearl Taylor Hart wrote this poem while languishing in her Yuma Territorial Prison cell after being sentenced to serve five years—not for robbing the Globe stagecoach on May 29, 1899, but for taking the Colt .45 from driver Henry Bacon. While her poetry lacked any symmetry or syntactic finesse, her creative endeavor played across the country's newspapers as another chapter in Pearl's already checkered and often fictionalized history. She memorialized her famous stage robbery in these lines and relished the fame, albeit no fortune, that followed.

Many of the facts about Pearl Hart are skewed by her own vivid imagination. Once she tasted the thrill of celebrity, she continually elaborated on her stage-robbing escapade. Journalists picked up every tale she told, and many accepted her utterances as gospel truth.

Over time historians have pieced together some of the facts of Pearl Hart's life, but since she freely twisted her history to suit an immediate situation, some truths may never be known.

And although there are those who believe the lady outlaw was an ignorant morphine addict and harlot, in reality, she was a high-energy, educated young woman who happened to fall in love with the wrong man.

Born in Lindsay, Ontario, Canada, in 1871, Pearl Taylor was described by a childhood friend as "very pretty . . . lithe-some, blithe, and witty, gushing with fun and jollity, also a wonderful dancer." But, apparently, "She was too amorous, accepted too many dates with handsome young men, which finally caused her undoing."

Pearl attended boarding school until, and at age sixteen, she eloped with a handsome, smooth-talking gambler and some-times bartender, probably named Frank Hart. The young couple seemed happy enough at first, but when Hart's earnings took a turn for the worse, which they often did, so did his temper.

Through the years Pearl left her abusive husband on numer-ous occasions, but she would always return after he plaintively apologized for his violent behavior. She could not resist his handsome face and beguiling words of endearment.

The couple reunited in 1893 and traveled to Chicago to attend the World's Columbian Exposition. While her husband earned a few dollars as a barker, Pearl visited Buffalo Bill's Wild West Show and became enamored with the excitement and lure of the untamed west. When Hart mistreated her once again, she hopped a train that dropped her off in the coal-mining community of Trinidad, Colorado.

Pearl may have arrived in Colorado on the arm of piano player Dan Bandman. Other reports indicate she arrived alone and worked as a domestic, hotel maid, or cook. Then there are those who insist she had already acquired a fondness for morphine and made her living as a soiled dove in a bawdy house.

Pearl refused to elaborate on these years. In an interview with *Cosmopolitan* magazine in 1899, she said, "I do not care to dwell on this period of my life. It is sufficient to say that I went from one city to another until some time later I arrived in Phoenix." Before leaving Trinidad, she gave birth to a son.

After she reconciled with her husband in 1895, the couple lived in Phoenix, enjoyed wedded bliss for about three years, and had a daughter. After a particularly violent fight that left Pearl unconscious, she again left Hart, going east to work as a domestic. She sent her children to live with her mother.

Hart persuaded Pearl to return to him once more and the couple spent some time in Tucson before he supposedly left to fight in the Spanish-American War. Relocating to Phoenix, Pearl declared she hoped the Spanish would "get him."

She moved into a tent on the banks of the Gila River and cooked for miners in the Mammoth area. When her health deteriorated, Joe Boot, a sometimes miner who had befriended the struggling woman, suggested the two of them try their luck around Globe, a seemingly more profitable mining district. She found work as a cook in a Globe boardinghouse until one of the larger quarries closed and she was again destitute.

Around this time Pearl received a letter from her brother claiming he was in a scrape and needed money. She sent him what she could, but shortly thereafter another letter arrived saying her mother, who now lived in Ohio, was dying and wanted to see her daughter one last time. With no funds Pearl was frantic to get to the woman who had never given up on her wayward daughter, the woman who watched over her children.

Although Pearl said in her *Cosmopolitan* interview that Boot "proposed that we rob the Globe stage," she later left a note saying she "forced Joe Boot at the point of my gun to help me hold up the stage. It was my fault, not his. He loved me and did as I said. If he had not, I sure would have killed him and he knew it too." She went on to say she would have done anything to get to her dying mother—including robbing a stage.

As Boot and Pearl fled after the robbery, they planned to head for Benson, hop a train, and travel whichever way the rails were running. Instead they entered Benson as prisoners of Sheriff Truman. He transported them by rail to Casa Grande, then by buckboard to the Florence jail, arriving with his passengers on June 4.

After Pearl tried to fake her suicide by throwing talcum powder in her face, Truman decided his facility was not suitable for female occupants. He bought Pearl a proper dress and hat to take the place of her masculine attire and escorted her to the Tucson jail to await trial.

But Pearl had no intention of waiting for the courts to decide her fate. She was on a mission to see her "darling old gray haired mother." On October 12, 1899, after luring a love-struck, incarcerated bicycle thief named Edward Hogan (or Ed Sherwood) into her plan of escape, Pearl wiggled out of a hole her paramour had cut in her makeshift cell and the two escaped into the night.

In the note she left behind in the Tucson jail confessing it was her idea to rob the stagecoach, she also warned, "If she [her mother] has died since my arrest God pity those who kept me from her. I shall have no pity and shall devote my entire life to killing all who detained me."

Pearl Hart
Courtesy of the Arizona Historical Society/Tucson, AHS #9183

The fugitives clung between two rail cars on the eastbound train out of Tucson headed for Lordsburg, New Mexico, where they parted ways. By the time Pearl reached Deming, her whereabouts were well known to US Marshal George A. Scarborough, who kept her under surveillance until Hogan/ Sherwood reappeared. After arresting the pair, he notified Tucson authorities to come and get their wandering renegades.

As she boarded the train in Deming for the return trip to Tucson, Pearl regaled the crowd that came to see her with capricious stories about her famed stagecoach heist. Thus the elaborate saga of her days as a lady bandit began to multiply and merge fact with fiction.

Pearl's trial commenced in Florence in November 1899, before the Honorable Fletcher M. Doan. She batted her eyes at the jurors and shed a few tears while relating the sad tale of her dying mother. Purportedly, she even evoked the suffrage movement into her pathetic pleas, claiming she would never "consent to be tried under a law which my sex had no voice in making." And it worked. Ten minutes after the jurors received the case, they returned a verdict of not guilty for the darling Pearl of the West.

Furious with her acquittal, Judge Doan immediately had her rearrested and charged with stealing the stage driver's pistol. A new jury quickly found her guilty, and Doan sentenced her to five years in Yuma Territorial Prison, proclaiming it would take at least that long to alleviate her proclivity for robbing stagecoaches.

As the train carrying Pearl to prison passed through the small communities that lined the rails from Florence to Yuma, the *Coconino Sun* noted she could be seen "with a big cigar in her mouth rivaling the efforts of the locomotive to charge the atmosphere with smoke."

In the meantime Joe Boot was tried separately, found guilty of robbing the stagecoach, and sentenced to serve thirty years in Yuma Territorial Prison. Boot became a model prisoner. He was made a trustee and allowed to drive food wagons to work crews outside the prison walls. On February 6, 1901, he drove through the prison gates as usual and did not look back. He was never seen again.

Yuma Territorial Prison was home to several women before Pearl Hart, but she was certainly the most famous female inmate. Construction on the adobe and stone penitentiary began in 1875, and work continued on the edifice the entire thirty-four years of the prison's existence. Yuma citizens called the modern facility "the Country Club on the Colorado," protesting that prisoners basked in the luxurious setting along the banks of the Colorado River. Pearl might have disagreed with them as she languished in her caliche cell, where temperatures often registered well above 100 degrees.

In the spring of 1901, Pearl's sister, Mrs. C. P. Frizzell, visited her in Yuma. Mrs. Frizzell claimed she had written a play, *The Arizona Bandit*, detailing her sister's adventures and expected Pearl to star in the presentation after her release. However, no proof exists that the play was every performed.

In the fall of 1902, the female section of the prison was becoming exceedingly full as more women were invited to spend time in the Yuma facility. To alleviate the overcrowding, the prison superintendent recommended the release of Pearl Hart, along with seventeen-year-old Rosa Duran, who had served thirteen months of her three-year term for grand larceny. In a November 15 letter to the Board of Control, the superintendent also recommended that Pearl be ordered to "remain out of the Territory of Arizona for the term of her sentence." Two days later, the board approved the release of the two women.

The superintendent received several letters from Pearl's sister promising to pay the fare to Kansas City, Missouri, so Pearl could reunite with her family. She left Arizona on December 15, 1902.

But another scenario involving Pearl's release is much more damning to those entrusted with her care. In September 1956 journalist Bert Fireman reported in the *Arizona Republic* magazine that Pearl was pregnant when she was released from prison. According to Fireman, in 1954, after all individuals involved in the cover-up had died, George Smalley, secretary to Governor Alexander O. Brodie in 1902, claimed the prison superintendent had told Brodie that, according to the prison doctor, Pearl was pregnant. Supposedly, only three men had access to her cell: the governor, the superintendent, and a trustee. To avoid any scandal she was released with the stipulation that she leave Arizona.

No records have materialized confirming that Pearl Hart gave birth after her discharge from prison. In retrospect this account might be looked upon as yet another trick up Pearl's conniving sleeve to obtain an early release.

A few months later, while selling cigars in Kansas City, Pearl was arrested for "complicity with thieves." At the time she was using the name Mrs. L. P. Keele. After that, Pearl Hart disappeared from public view, at least for a while.

Sightings of Pearl continued to pop up as the years rolled along. In 1928 she may have returned to Tucson. Several people claimed they saw her hanging around the courthouse jail where she was once held on charges of robbing the Globe stage. She would have been about fifty-seven years old.

More substantial evidence that Pearl returned to Arizona lies in the history of Globe, Arizona, as told by Clara T. Woody in 1977. Woody served as census taker for Globe during the 1940s and claimed she met Pearl on several occasions. She said Pearl married rancher Calvin Bywater and lived quietly on the Dripping Springs Ranch, not far from Cane Springs Canyon, the scene of that long-ago stage robbery. If this was the notorious Pearl Hart, she never admitted her past. Until her death on December 30, 1955, Mrs. Calvin Bywater never used her first name, nor did she give any indication that she had lived an outlaw life.

Neither pistol nor pen gave Pearl Hart a life of respectability. Wherever she lies today, she will always be remembered as Arizona Territory's bandit queen, a woman of fact and fiction, fame and fascination, who was both adored and vilified.

Albert Wright
"Burt" Alvord
Bandit with a Badge

On the evening of September 9, 1899, Willcox, Arizona, Constable Burt Alvord, who was also a deputy sheriff for Cochise County, surveyed the poker hand in front of him and ordered another round of drinks at Schwertner's Saloon. He enjoyed hanging out with Willcox's local boys, even if the cards in front of him were not profitable tonight. His pleasant evening was suddenly disrupted when a messenger burst through the saloon door—bandits had robbed the Southern Pacific train at Cochise Station! Alvord jumped up, his six-foot frame towering above the gathering crowd. Visibly upset that someone had moved in on his territory, he immediately rounded up a posse and headed to the crime scene.

His two deputies, Billy Stiles and Bill Downing, joined the posse at Cochise Station. He ordered Stiles to take some men and head north, and Downing to take the southern route. Alvord led a third group toward the Chiricahua Mountains. The bandits had been clever though. They had followed a rock-hard riverbed, exhausted of rain for months, leaving few hoof prints to follow. Alvord finally ordered the men back to town without finding any trace of the robbers.

Speculation grew as to who could have masterminded such a successful robbery. Almost a year passed before Willcox's own constable, the tall, sometimes ruthless but fun-loving Albert Wright "Burt" Alvord was fingered as ringleader of a group of men who straddled both sides of the law.

Alvord certainly started out on the right side of justice. His father, after bringing the family from California to Tombstone in 1880, often served as the town's justice of the peace. Born Albert Wright Alvord in Susanville, California, on September 11, 1867, Alvord was a young teen when he arrived in Tombstone. He may have witnessed the O. K. Corral gunfight on October 26, 1881, as he sometimes worked at the corral, sweeping out stables, tending horses, and making repairs.

Alvord received most of his education on the streets of Tombstone. He could shoot billiards with the best of the cowboys, and his whittling was of expert quality. He loved to play practical jokes and often resolved differences from his pranks with his fists, sometimes a gun. He particularly enjoyed a good bar fight.

In 1886 Cochise County Sheriff John H. Slaughter enlisted Alvord as deputy sheriff. Slaughter knew the twenty-year-old could handle himself with a gun and often acted on instinct. Frequently, the two lawmen surprised sleeping bandits by shucking their boots before sneaking into enemy camps. Although careful to note that they warned suspected culprits to surrender before firing, and insisting the men almost always reached for their guns, Slaughter and Alvord brought in few live prisoners.

Alvord earned a reputation as a hard-riding, quick-shooting lawman. He took part in such notable events as the search for suspects in the 1889 Wham Paymaster Robbery and the attempted capture of notorious killer Augustine Chacón, one of the most feared desperadoes in Arizona Territory.

Alvord discovered that hunting down outlaws sometimes brought lucrative profits. After killing a horse thief, he confiscated the bandit's cartridge/money belt, including $500 in gold. Sometimes he rode with another illegal equine collector, Eduardo Lopez, stealing Papago ponies and selling them for about $10 each. Sheriff Slaughter usually ignored his deputy's indiscretions.

Alvord served as deputy to several sheriffs after John Slaughter. "He was not one to mess with," according to historian Don Chaput, "but good to have around if force was a consideration." He knew the surrounding terrain as well as he knew how much whiskey was behind the bar. If things got out of hand during one of his practical jokes, the sheriff at the time was inclined to look the other way and let him have his fun.

He almost got himself killed in 1890 when he and Biddy Doyle played one prank too close to the vest. After fixing a wrestling match, the two men hightailed it out of Bisbee with the money purse and an angry mob close behind. Another time, he and Max Marks, after enjoying a lengthy session in a Bisbee saloon, telegraphed the *Tombstone Epitaph* that the "bodies of Marks and Alvord will arrive this afternoon." Two coffins waited in somber silence outside the O. K. Corral stage stop. As passengers departed the stage, so did Alvord and Marks. "Sure our bodies arrived," they said. "We never go out without 'em."

In 1894 gold was discovered in the tiny town of Pearce, about twenty miles east of Tombstone. With the mines came saloons, dance halls, and unruly miners hell-bent on having a good time. In 1896 Alvord became deputy constable of Pearce, and before long the little community was as peaceful as a cow pasture. He married Lola Ochoa and bought a house in town and a ranch in the Dragoon Mountains. For a while his days straddling both sides of the law lay behind him.

Alvord's reputation for cleaning up towns spread. In June 1897 he was asked to take on the job of deputy constable at Willcox. A month later Willcox's constable resigned, and Alvord took over the position.

While Pearce's problems stemmed from celebrating miners, Willcox entertained tough-riding cowboys. On one occasion a bunch of Friday-night buckaroos caught Alvord and his deputies off guard at Kasper Hauser's saloon. As they locked the lawmen in the basement for the night, the entertainment escalated upstairs.

The next morning cowboy Billy King let Alvord out and apologized for his part in the prank. King even offered to buy Alvord a new hat since his was demolished in the night's revelry. Alvord rubbed his shiny bald head, and, although somewhat aggravated the joke was on him this time, he slapped King on the back and escorted him out the saloon door. Shots rang out. Alvord returned to the saloon alone, gun in hand, claiming he killed King in self-defense. No charges were filed against Willcox's tough new constable.

In early 1899 Cochise County Sheriff Scott White again made Alvord a deputy. Between his constable job in Willcox and his job as Cochise County deputy sheriff, Alvord enjoyed authority across most of southeastern Arizona and acquired as many enemies as he did friends. To protect his back, he made Billy Stiles his deputy in Willcox, and sometimes enlisted the help of Bill Downing, a man of questionable background, and Matt Burts, a barfly.

Alvord managed Willcox so well, he was spending more of his time in local saloons rather than hunting down outlaws. With little money to spend (lawmen made paltry salaries), he devised a scheme to rob the Southern Pacific train at Cochise Station.

Alvord figured the payroll for the Pearce mines should be on board the westbound Southern Pacific train the night of September 9, 1899. He knew the engine had to slow to a crawl as it climbed the steep grade outside Cochise Station, just a few miles from Willcox. It was the perfect spot for a holdup. He had no trouble convincing his three deputies—Stiles, Downing, and Burts—to perform the heist.

Alvord and his deputies broke into a local mercantile to obtain the dynamite they needed. They struck a nearby mining camp to stock up on explosive caps and fuses. Downing supplied the horses. They were ready.

The train ascended the hill and let out one final exhaustive sigh of steam as it came to a stop beneath the water tank. As engineer C. A. Richardson readied the powerful machine to take on nourishment, he was suddenly facing the wrong end of a six-gun. Burts ordered Richardson and the fireman to uncouple the engine and move the mail and express cars away from the rest of the train toward a cluster of desert brush. Stiles disarmed the mail clerk and Wells Fargo agent.

Down the track Downing emerged from the bushes and ordered Richardson to take the engine several hundred yards away from the mail and express cars. The men placed a thundering amount of dynamite in the two cars, set the charge, and ducked for cover. The cars exploded hundreds of feet in the air with cash, gold coins, and jewelry blowing across the desert, creating a bountiful rainfall of wealth. The bandits quickly gathered the loot, jumped on horses secreted in the brush, and rode hard for parts unknown.

Meanwhile, Burt Alvord played poker in a Willcox saloon.

Even today, no one agrees how much money and gold was on the train; some figures ran as high as $80,000. Since the Pearce payroll was on an earlier train, chances are the men realized much less than they anticipated. It was later determined that Alvord distributed a small portion of the loot to his accomplices, but most of it was never found.

Feeling flush after his first victory at robbing trains, Alvord struck again. This time, the scheme was a little more complicated, but the stakes just as lucrative. As before, he would take no role in the actual robbery, showing himself around town while the action happened far from his presence.

Alvord enlisted Stiles to waylay Wells Fargo agent Jeff Milton in Nogales. He did not want Milton on board the targeted train out of Nogales to Benson. Milton was a crack shot, and no savvy outlaw dared challenge him. At the last minute, however, Milton was called to replace the scheduled agent. He forgot to tell Stiles who was waiting for him in Nogales.

The night of February 14, 1900, was as dark as a gunslinger's soul. Five men huddled against the cold deep in the Dragoon Mountains. Three of them, Bob Brown and brothers George and Lewis Owens, were ranch hands. Bravo Juan Yoas and Three-Fingered Jack Dunlap already had accumulated criminal records. Only the promise of a train full of gold kept the men warm.

Burt Alvord was at his usual post—lining up drinks at a Benson saloon.

On the morning of February 15, the New Mexico & Arizona train left Nogales as scheduled, except for the presence of Jeff Milton instead of the regular Wells Fargo agent. It made one scheduled stop in Fairbank, about twenty miles south of Benson, arriving near sundown. As passengers filled the platform, no one paid attention to the five men mingling with the crowd.

Bob Brown and Lewis Owens entered the engine's cab without incident, disarming the engineer and fireman.

When Jeff Milton opened the express car doors, no one was more surprised to see him than the three desperadoes who had made their way to the front of the crowd. But with little hesitation, they demanded Milton drop his weapon. Milton hesitated to shoot into the crowd until one of the bandits fired a shot through the agent's hat. In one quick move, Milton grabbed his rifle and opened fire.

The bandits blasted the rail car, wounding Milton as they boarded. They searched frantically for the keys to the safe. Milton, barely conscious, managed to grab his shotgun and hit Dunlap full force; some of the buckshot ended up in Yoas's rump.

Aware the gunfight had aroused more attention than they could handle and with no luck finding the keys to the safe, the men dragged the mortally wounded Dunlap off the train, grabbed their horses, and fled, richer by less than $50. They split up as they ran, abandoning Dunlap by the side of the road.

The next day the posse found Dunlap next to a blackened cactus. He had tried to start a fire but only succeeded in burning the plant as well as himself. The dying man survived the trip to Tombstone and lived a few more days, plenty of time to finger the culprits in the Fairbank heist, including the two who were nowhere near the robbery site—Burt Alvord and Billy Stiles. Dunlap also told all he knew about the Cochise Station robbery, again naming Alvord as the leader and implicating Stiles, Matt Burts, and Bill Downing.

The suspects were rounded up and jailed in Tombstone's tiny facility. Only Stiles remained free after he sang loud and fast to authorities about his part in the two robberies and named Alvord as ringleader. Alvord vehemently denied his involvement in both incidents. He did not relish sitting in a lockup with criminals he had arrested, and he had no intention of staying there.

On April 8 Stiles walked into the jailhouse and asked to speak to Alvord. Afterward, as the jailer led Alvord back to his cell, Stiles stuck a gun in the officer's side and relieved him of the jail keys. Alvord unlocked the cell doors, but only Bravo Juan Yoas walked out—the rest chose to take their chances at trial. Grabbing guns and rifles, the trio headed for the door, but the jailer made one last attempt to stop them receiving a bullet in the leg as the trio fled.

About a week later Sheriff Scott White received a package in the mail. In it were the keys to the Tombstone jail and a note from the three escapees: "Tell the boys we are all well and eating regular." Alvord treated the whole episode as another of his pranks.

For three months the men were on the run. Stiles finally headed to his home in Casa Grande, leaving the other two riding toward Mexico. During their stay south of the border, Alvord and Yoas may have worked as armed guards in Mexican mines, since both were fluent in Spanish.

In 1902 Arizona Ranger Captain Burton C. Mossman set out to capture the killer Augustine Chacón and needed Alvord's help to bring in the desperado. Alvord may have ridden with Chacón at one time and the killer trusted him. When Alvord met up with Mossman in Mexico, he had been on the run for two years and was nursing a broken wrist. Mossman promised to recommend a lighter sentence for Alvord if he helped capture Chacón.

Alvord was ready to return to the states and once he put Mossman in touch with Chacón, he fled north. A week later, Alvord surrendered to Sheriff Del Lewis in the border town of Naco.

On December 1, 1902, Alvord appeared before a Tombstone judge. His attorney argued that Bill Downing had been found not guilty of the train heist because a jury thought the mandatory death penalty too harsh a judgment for robbing a train. The court agreed and ordered charges against Alvord dismissed.

Albert Wright "Burt" Alvord, circa 1897
Courtesy of the Arizona Historical Society/Tucson, AHS #13878

Other allegations still loomed however—the jailbreak and wounding of the Tombstone jailer, plus far more serious federal charges of tampering with the US mail during the Cochise Station robbery. By December 8 Alvord was back in jail but paid his bail and walked out after serving eight days.

In July 1903 a grand jury indicted Alvord on six counts of tampering with the US mail. Bail was set at $9,000. This time, the man who had initiated the robbery of two money-laden trains offered up no hard cash to pay for his release.

Stiles fled rather than testify against Alvord, but was recaptured. Not wanting the two desperadoes in the same jail, authorities sent Alvord to Phoenix to await trial while Stiles hung out in the Tucson facility. Both men were transported to Tombstone a few days before their December 10 trial date.

Unexpectedly, Alvord withdrew his "not guilty" plea and pled "guilty" to robbing the US mail. The court dismissed five additional charges against him, reducing his sentence to two years in Yuma Territorial Prison.

While Alvord waited to be transported to Yuma, he languished in the aging Tombstone jail with his old pal Stiles. The men wasted no time letting themselves out. On the evening of December 15, Alvord and Stiles slithered through a hole they had dug in the jail's adobe wall and walked away.

After stealing a couple of horses, they made one stop before heading toward the border. With their horses hidden behind a dry goods store and their guns drawn, the two escapees rapped on the shop's back door. Young Percy Bowden, who would later become a lawman, "opened the door to find two men with guns drawn and pointing in my direction." The men ordered Bowden to bring them warm clothes and supplies.

After hearing the list of chores the boy did each day—milking sixteen cows and delivering milk before school, sweeping the store, and cleaning windows—they suggested their line of work was more lucrative but "might not last as long if the law caught up with them . . ." They handed the boy two $20 gold pieces and disappeared into the night.

By January 1904 a $500 reward hung over each man's head. Accused of several robberies in the Sonora area, Alvord later claimed he had nothing to do with any of them. One of these thefts included $8,000 in gold bullion that was never recovered.

On February 19 Alvord and Stiles were spotted hanging out at a ranch west of Naco, Sonora. Arizona Rangers surprised the two outlaws, severely wounding Alvord. Stiles escaped.

On March 3 Alvord entered Yuma Territorial Prison. He was released sometime in early October 1905. For a while, he lived with a sister in Los Angeles, then disappeared. Many believe he ended up on the Caribbean island of Barbados, changed his name to Tom Wright, and died of fever in 1910. At the time, he had in his possession about $800 in gold, which was released to his sister.

In 1938 two of Alvord's nieces filed a note with the Arizona Historical Society stating their uncle had died on a small island off the Atlantic coast of Panama, "about the Fall of 1910."

Burt Alvord turned his back on justice, discarding his badge for a robber's six-gun. As one of Arizona Territory's most notorious bad men, he is remembered more for his lawlessness than his success in bringing justice to a handful of unruly western towns.

Cecil Creswell
The Gray-Haired Lady Rustler

As the sun dipped below the horizon, rancher John Thompson headed his horse toward home. He took his usual route but knew he had to keep a sharp eye out for his neighbor, who had a habit of taking potshots at anyone passing too close to her property. Cecil Creswell was a crack shot and Thompson wanted no part in quarreling with a lady, although he might argue she was more a witch than a proper woman.

The gunshots came quickly, nearly knocking Thompson off his horse. As he ducked low and spurred his mount into a hasty gallop, he grabbed his saddle horn for balance and realized it had been shot clean off. This was not the first time he had narrowly missed getting hit with a barrage of bullets from Cecil's trusty .30-30 rifle, and he probably muttered a few choice words for his pistol-packing neighbor as he hightailed it out of shooting range.

No cowboy in northern Arizona wanted to cross Cecil Creswell. Her petite stature and mop of gray hair belied her ability to perform just about any task on her small ranch, and she could outshoot most men in the area. She had lived on her Winslow, Arizona, property since 1924, gaining a reputation as a hard worker who kept to herself and asked little of others. She also earned the title of cattle rustler, as she occasionally pilfered a cow or two from her neighbors.

Olive Dove Van Zoast, born on the family farm in Olivet, South Dakota, sometime between 1892 and 1901, left home

131

around the age of fourteen and seemed to disconnect herself from her family for the remainder of her life. No one knows how or where she acquired the name Cecil.

Somewhere in her travels she signed on with the Fred Harvey Company, known for its chain of railroad eating houses and later hotels along the Atchison, Topeka and Santa Fe Railway lines, to work as a Harvey Girl.

Mary Elizabeth Jane Colter, chief architect and interior designer for the Fred Harvey Company, completed La Posada (The Inn) in Winslow in 1930, and Cecil was one of many Harvey Girls hired to work in the plush lodging. Mary Colter designed many of the magnificent buildings at the Grand Canyon, but La Posada was considered one of her most detailed and elaborate edifices.

Cecil must have loved working in the opulent Spanish-style hacienda. The pink, two-story building contained seventy rooms and five suites. Pegged-oak planks lined the floors, ceilings were painted turquoise with gold and silver accents, and antique Spanish engravings splayed across the walls. Few buildings in the Southwest could compete with the grandeur of the plush hotel. It remains today a remembrance of long-ago days when traveling by train was considered a luxury, and it is still a focal point in the old railroad town of Winslow.

Founded in 1880, Winslow borders on the Navajo and Hopi Reservations in Navajo County, Arizona. In 1881 the first rail lines were laid through town by the Atlantic & Pacific Railroad. The addition of La Posada and the Harvey Girls put Winslow on the map as visitors flocked to the luxurious hotel.

Harvey Girls adhered to strict standards while employed with the Fred Harvey Company; they could not engage in any scandalous activity. Although their uniform dress changed slightly through the years, they were almost always clad in black and white. Long-sleeved blouses with high, stiff starched collars topped skirts rising no more than eight inches off the floor, revealing black stockings and shoes. Pristine, starched white aprons were changed immediately if stained. Hair had to be tied under a net with a white ribbon. The girls were forbidden to wear makeup or jewelry, and chewing gum was discouraged.

Cecil apparently accepted the rules and regulations of being a Harvey Girl, but whenever she had the chance, she shed her nun-like uniform for boots and Levi's and headed down to the horse barn to ride into the country unencumbered by the conventions of her job. One cowboy who knew her when she worked at La Posada recalled, "She was a pretty good rider."

According to the *Winslow Mail*, Cecil married several times. Her first husband, a railroad policeman, was imprisoned for bigamy. She then married George Creswell, and the couple settled in Tuba City, Arizona, where Creswell worked as a livestock inspector for the Bureau of Indian Affairs. Mary May Bailey, whose father ran trading posts on the nearby Navajo and Hopi Reservations, first met the couple in Tuba City and remembered Cecil as "very attractive, sort of blond hair and about 5 feet, 4 inches and slim. But she had a lot of strength and a lot of athletic ability. She was very friendly then and knew everyone and loved to go to dances."

In 1924 George Creswell died. Cecil, now in her late thirties, left Tuba City and moved onto a 160-acre parcel of bare land homesteaded by Creswell just outside of Winslow. She relied on no one as she poured cement for the foundation of her home and plastered the walls herself. She built a corral and dug a water tank for her cattle with only a pick and shovel. She hauled water from Clear Creek, about half a mile away.

She used both the Bar 3 Bar and Rafter 3 brands on her livestock. She could throw a hefty cow weighing several hundred pounds and brand it with no assistance. A forty-foot rock wall, built solely by Cecil, stood in front of her house that was protected by two large dogs even she could not control. Yet she could barely make ends meet and often subsisted on a scant plate of beans for supper.

For money, she occasionally worked as a hired hand on nearby ranches and could hold her own with other cowboys when it came to riding, roping, and wrangling. Her biggest passion was horses, and she often went into the mountains to catch wild mustangs, then broke them to ride. Her own horse, named Pig, was one of these big, untamed stallions.

Cecil's troubles escalated sometime in the 1940s. Some speculated she began to rustle cattle because she needed the food, while other opinions varied from just plain orneriness to downright thievery. When she started shooting at anyone approaching her property, her reputation as a menace and pilferer of fine beef escalated.

According to the women of Winslow, the men in the area were threatened by this independent, free-spirited woman, her sharp-shooting abilities and prowess with a horse, and the fact she dressed like a man. In contrast, the local women found the petite cowgirl a kind and gentle individual, "a perfect lady," according to Mary Bailey.

Cecil met her third husband, rancher Moon Mullens, sometime after arriving in Winslow. In the early 1940s Mullens died after being struck by lightning. Other romantic liaisons may have left Cecil with physical as well as emotional scars. She turned inward, wary, and reticent, even with her old friends.

"Cecil had some horrendous experience during this time," Mary Bailey believed, "something that profoundly changed her personality. She was always very guarded in her conversations. She would greet you if she met you on the street, but there was never any small talk."

Cecil only went into town when she could afford to buy supplies and would tie her horse, Pig, to a parking meter outside of Babbitt's Store, the general mercantile. The four Babbitt brothers—Edward, George, William, and Charles—arrived in Flagstaff from Cincinnati, Ohio, in 1886, establishing a trading company that eventually became one of northern Arizona's leading businesses for almost one hundred years. They branched out into towns like Winslow, trading cattle, sheep, and general merchandise, while bartering with Native tribes for jewelry, blankets, and baskets.

Cecil often swapped fresh beef in return for groceries. Usually the cow was not from her stock but borrowed from a neighbor. And if she could not find a stray cow, she sometimes substituted burro meat, proclaiming it to be fresh beef right off the range.

She appropriated a bull from local rancher T. C. Kaufman. Trying to disguise her ill-gotten stock, she colored the bull's light tan coat with henna dye, which turned the hide a deep red. She then branded it with her Rafter 3 brand. For over a year, Kaufman rode past that red bull grazing on Cecil's property without recognizing his own prized bovine.

When her cattle trough failed to hold water, she discovered Fred Stubblefield's fishing boat down by the creek and had Pig haul it back to the ranch. She filled the dinghy with water, providing a fine substitute for the arid ditch for years. Not until after Cecil died did Stubblefield realize what had happened to his boat.

Most ranchers looked the other way when Cecil stole a cow here and there, assuming she needed the meat to survive. Winslow law had no desire to go after a woman who could shoot straighter than most of them, and the local sheriff of Navajo County, L. Ben Pearson, allegedly brought her boxes of food and clothing to help her out.

But times were getting tougher. In 1949 she was arrested for shooting at one of her neighbors, rancher Sam Duran, and placed under a peace bond. Three years later, in July 1952, she was fined $300 for cutting down a fence and trespassing. The following month, she was charged with cruelty to animals for shooting a bull belonging to rancher John Thompson, fined $150, and given a suspended jail sentence.

The potshots she took at neighboring ranchers who ventured too close to her property soon became a source of unpleasantness to everyone within shooting distance. Cowboys repairing fence lines complained that they had to fend off the lady sniper all day, ducking and weaving to avoid being hit. John Thompson claimed she once heckled him as he rode by. "I just kept on riding like I didn't hear her," he said. "Then she started firing and those big old bullets went past so close I could have reached out and caught them."

"She was a troublemaker," Thompson declared. But he also knew, "You can't fight a woman. You just as well fight your hat."

"[S]he was a criminal, a cattle rustler, a mean, rough old lady," said Dale Hancock who, as a teenager, had run into Cecil while building fences for Thompson. Hancock claimed Cecil would "shoot at us nearly every day, usually from about a quarter of a mile away. That's a long ways, I know, but it's close enough when somebody is shooting at you. I can tell you she kept us scared all the time."

Yet Mary Bailey knew, "If she wanted to hit the men, she would have. Cecil was a perfect shot." Even the local jackrabbits were wary of Cecil's prowess with a gun, and many of them ended up on her dinner table as a tasty meal.

Neighbor Stella Hughes found Cecil a "good neighbor, but I think Cecil should have been born at an earlier time. She thought of herself as a woman of the Wild West, and I think she would have been perfectly at home in the times of Pearl Hart and Calamity Jane."

John Thompson finally had enough after Cecil shot off his saddle horn. He filed a complaint and had a warrant issued for her arrest.

During this time, an eighteen-month investigation by the Arizona Livestock Sanitary Board was under way to examine cattle rustling in the area. On March 4, 1954, Cecil was charged with rustling cattle and horses.

The following morning Sheriff Pearson and Deputy James E. Brisendine headed out to arrest the gray-haired, sixty-plus-year-old woman.

Cecil asked if she could change her clothes before going into town and invited the men into her house. Deputy Brisendine, obviously impressed with the neatness of the little ranch, noted the walls of her home ". . . were covered with pictures that she had painted . . . landscapes, desert scenes, and pictures of wildlife that were absolutely fantastic."

Before long Arden McFadden, chief livestock inspector of the Sanitary Board, along with inspectors C. B. Griffin and Harvey

Randal, plus several local ranchers, showed up to investigate the property for stolen goods. Cecil agreed that they could look around, claiming she had raised all her livestock from calves.

Although the cattle all bore Cecil's Bar 3 Bar brand, Oscar Reid, one of the ranchers with the inspectors, claimed that some of the calves were his and should show the 4 Dart brand on the left front quarters. The calves were roped and the hair clipped at the left shoulder. Sure enough, the 4 Dart brand appeared. The investigation uncovered twenty-one stolen cows.

Faced with arrest, Cecil asked if she could return to her house to use the bathroom before being hauled off to the Winslow jail. With no matron or woman deputy along, she was allowed to go into the house alone. As soon as she disappeared, Deputy Brisendine knew he had made a mistake. "She had no sooner left the corral," he said, "when it dawned on me that she had no bathroom in her house. She didn't even have running water on the ranch.

"I was expecting to hear the crack of her .30-30 Carbine at any second, and from that distance, she could pick us off one at a time."

When the shot rang out, the deputy knew "[W]e will have to shoot her or she will shoot us."

But no other gunfire was exchanged. Instead, a deadly silence settled over Cecil's little ranch house. Sheriff Pearson shouted for Cecil to come out but received no reply. He and the deputy cautiously approached the front door. On orders to kick down the door, the deputy "was not eager to do this because we could be looking at the bad end of her .30-30 rifle when we got inside." The sheriff hammered down the door. Brisendine described the scene:

Cecil Creswell
Courtesy of the Winslow [Arizona] Historical Society/Old Trails Museum

[W]e found the most heartbreaking thing that one could imagine. Cecil had put the barrel of the gun into her mouth and pulled the trigger. . . . She had completely decapitated herself, her head was severed from her body, and blood and hair was all over the place, even on the ceiling. She was kneeling on a chair that was near her bed like she had been praying.

If Cecil had only known that we had no intention of sending her to prison, but was going to make arrangements for her to go into a supervised mental ward in Phoenix, which was extremely nice, where she could visit, and live out her life in peace.

Outside, more evidence piled up against the elderly cowgirl. Along with the mismarked yearlings found in her corral, the men found an old gray mare belonging to one of the ranchers, then discovered a lime pit filled with at least a dozen cow carcasses.

Seven days after her death, Cecil was buried in Winslow's Desert View Cemetery. According to her obituary in the *Winslow Mail*, it was a simple service "attended by a small number of . . . her friends . . ."

Feelings ran hot and heavy around town after Cecil's death. According to cowboy Nelson Goldsberry, "The old-timers in Winslow were so outraged at Cecil's death that they threatened to kill the officers." Yet John Thompson could not contain his relief that his archenemy was gone. "She was a witch," he proclaimed, "about as worse a witch as you could meet."

Deputy Brisendine returned to Cecil's house and discovered not one bit of food in the entire place, not even salt or pepper. While searching through her belongings, he uncovered a cache of photographs and letters under rugs and inside the walls.

Cecil had placed her bed in the kitchen. Beneath it, she had stashed a bundle of old jeans wrapped up in barbed wire. A brand new washing machine sat unused, as she had no running water to the house. All her furniture was marked with the Rafter 3 brand. An array of manuscripts was uncovered, western stories and poetry she had written during her lifetime. A bank statement showing a closed account back in 1951 was the only evidence of money—not one cent was found in the house.

Eventually a sister was notified of Cecil's death. Ruth Moore had not seen her sister for over twenty years, and although there was no love lost between the siblings, she arrived in Winslow to check on Cecil's property. Cecil had willed her ranch and all her personal property to her friend, attorney Dewey McCauley. Uncomfortable about keeping property he felt belonged to the family, McCauley returned everything to Ruth. Ironically, Ruth sold Cecil's ranch to her archenemy, rancher John Thompson.

Cecil Creswell was a cattle and horse rustler. She was also a woman in a desperate situation. With no one to turn to, no one she trusted, she survived as only she knew how—with her gun, her grit, and her wits. No one messed with the gray-haired lady from Winslow.

Yuma Territorial Prison
The Hilltop Hacienda

On July 1, 1876, the first inmates walked through the gate of
Yuma Territorial Prison. They knew the place well, as they
had been part of the crew that constructed Arizona Territory's
first penitentiary. William H. Hall sported identification No. 1.
Sentenced to serve a life term for second-degree murder, Hall
actually spent nine years in Yuma Prison before receiving a pardon in 1884. Yet he must have liked this new adobe and stone
facility, because he returned to serve two more terms.

In Yuma Prison's thirty-four years of operation, 3,069 prisoners arrived at its entry gate, or sally port, twenty-nine of them
women. The new facility, sitting just across the Colorado River
from the original Fort Yuma, was touted as one of the plushest
penal institutions at the time, and many thought the inmates lived
much higher on the proverbial hog than some of the local towns-
folk. An August 24, 1890, *Arizona Republican* account detailing
the amenities of the modern facility found it "delightfully located
on a hill overlooking the town . . . hemmed in by rivers and open
valleys . . . the surroundings healthful and the elevation catches
refreshing and invigorating breezes. The temperature is never
very high and the nights are nearly always cool and pleasant."

According to the newspaper report, the cost of running
the new facility ran as much as $50,000 a year for about 143
prisoners. The article noted that the superintendent's house,
"furnished by the Territory, is long on champagne glasses and
short on water goblets, [which] may explain matters."

This hilltop hacienda should have stood within the parameters of the city of Phoenix, but a couple of astute Yuma politicians saw the economic advantages of having a prison in their vicinity and took measures to ensure its placement in southwestern Arizona.

The Fifth Territorial Legislature passed a bill establishing the prison in 1868, but funds were not forthcoming and plans for the building stagnated until the Eighth Territorial Legislature met in 1875. Yuma County Representatives José Maria Redondo and R. B. Kelly stealthily removed any reference in the bill to Phoenix as the city of choice for the prison and inserted the name Yuma as the town of preference. The bill was brought quickly and quietly before the Legislature, and bonds were approved for construction of the penitentiary. Before anyone realized the site selected was the sleepy town of Yuma, with a population of only a few hundred, Governor Anson P. K. Safford signed the bill establishing Yuma Territorial Prison.

Those who spent any time within the confines of the penal institution might argue with the popular notion that the facility sported a country club atmosphere. The initial twenty cells carved from the rocky hillside allowed little ventilation—yet cold winter winds whipped mercilessly through the enclosure, while the summer sun baked prisoners as they sought even a hint of shade within the confines of their stifling cubicles.

Each cell contained two rows of wooden bunk beds, a chamber pot, and an iron ring cemented into the floor to fetter a prisoner if necessary. The roof leaked and sewage backed up. The wooden bunks were plagued with bedbugs that enjoyed a tasty meal each night at the expense of the prisoners, so iron bunks were finally installed in 1902 to alleviate the infestation.

Those who disobeyed prison rules by cooking in the yard, refusing to work, fighting, using foul language, talking in cells after taps, or getting drunk on bay rum acquired for "tonsorial purposes" ended up in solitary confinement, a hole in the wall better known as the "snake den." The fifteen-by-fifteen-foot room dug into the hillside let in little light, except through a small ventilation shaft in the ceiling. Disobedient prisoners, stripped to their underwear and restricted to bread and water once a day, usually remained shackled in the snake den for three to four days. Those who attempted to escape from the penitentiary served about eleven days.

Horror tales abound about the snake den. One legend suggests that prison guards tormented those in solitary by dropping rattlesnakes and scorpions through the ventilation shaft. Unable to determine where the vermin came from in the darkness, the inmates blamed the guards, even though the creatures could have wandered in from the desert of their own accord.

Another story set the citizens of Yuma on edge. While preparing for a tour by a group of townswomen, the prison superintendent ordered everything cleaned spotless, including the ventilation shaft above the snake den. As the women entered the dark cell, a hoard of scorpions fell to the floor in front of the visiting entourage, probably dislodged from their hiding place in the cleaning frenzy. The women spread the word that the prison was a breeding place for all sorts of unwanted creatures.

Every convict received a bath and a shave upon entering Yuma Prison. Dressed in the black-and-gray or black-and-yellow striped uniform of the day, which changed to denim in 1892 when Levi Strauss won the bid to make prison clothing, an inmate was allowed to retain an extra pair of trousers plus two changes of underwear, socks, and handkerchiefs. He could have

Yuma Territorial Prison, circa 1890
Courtesy of the Arizona Historical Society/Tucson, AHS #91379

two combs, a toothbrush and toothpick, one pair of shoes, and a ration of tobacco. He received two sheets and pillowcases to make up his straw-tick mattress. He could keep his own stash of books. After his vital statistics were recorded and he received a prison number, he was placed in a chair with a mirror resting on his shoulder, which allowed him to be photographed from the front as well as at profile in the same picture.

All prisoners worked, whether it was laboring on the rock pile, making adobe bricks, working on the prison farm, cutting lumber in the wood yard, or serving in the kitchen or laundry. The tailor shop was particular busy, with inmates sewing clothing and shoes for prisoners along with civilian suits for departing parolees and clothing sold to the Insane Asylum of Arizona (now Arizona State Hospital), which opened in Phoenix in 1887. Some learned trades such as blacksmithing or carpentry.

By 1900 there was little left of the rock pile, and the wood industry proved unprofitable.

The prison farm, at one time over two thousand acres and touted for helping to reduce the economic load of feeding the inmates, was abandoned after five years of long winter droughts and periodic flooding by the Colorado River.

With beef a plentiful commodity in the cattle ranching community of Yuma, prisoners could expect meat at almost every meal—boiled, roasted, or stewed—along with staples such as bacon and beans, bread, and coffee. The cost of feeding a prisoner ran about thirty cents a day.

Inmates with good records could become trustees and often left the prison confines to work on city projects such as paving and repairing roads. Some found the taste of freedom a little too tempting and disappeared for good.

Spare time was limited, but detainees could play cards, though gambling was prohibited. By 1900 classes were initiated to teach English, Spanish, German, arithmetic, grammar, writing, spelling, composition, and music. Clergy from Yuma churches faithfully conducted religious services at the walled facility.

Craftsmanship was encouraged, and some of the inmates' artistic endeavors produced intricate, often exquisite items such as inlaid wooden boxes, horsehair braiding, silver and onyx work, saddle making, even lace tatting and scrimshaw. Several times each year the prison opened its gate to the public, allowing them to purchase these handmade items. The prisoners kept two-thirds of their earnings; the rest went into the coffers of the territory.

One of the first libraries built in Arizona belonged to Yuma Prison. Madora Ingalls, wife of Captain Frank S. Ingalls, the fourth prison superintendent, started the library in 1883. The long room tunneled about fifty feet into the rocky hillside and boasted over fifteen hundred volumes, plus an almost equal number of magazines and newspapers, most obtained through donations. Yuma citizens also enjoyed the benefits of the new library for a fee of twenty-five cents, with the proceeds providing additional materials. The library was later moved to a larger, separate building on the prison grounds.

Twenty-six men escaped from Yuma Prison. Many more tried and failed. Those attempts usually resulted in dead men on both sides of the law.

Although dangerous, guard jobs were highly sought after, as the $75 monthly pay was a good salary at the time. The sixteen men who held the job of superintendent during the prison's duration earned $250 a month.

An imposing Lowell Battery, an improved version of the Gatling Gun, stood above the main guard tower always aimed out across the prison grounds, keeping most prisoners at bay. Four barrels revolved and fired in rapid succession, having a devastating effect on any outbreak. It took two men to operate the commanding machine.

During one prison break, librarian Madora Ingalls saw only one man struggling to operate the powerful machine. Disregarding bullets that whizzed dangerously close to her head, she raced to assist the lone gunman as he aimed the massive weapon at the fleeing convicts.

The most dramatic break occurred in October 1887. Seven prisoners captured Superintendent Thomas Gates and ordered him to open the sally port. As the men escaped, Gates ordered the guards to fire. One of the prisoners pointed a pistol at Gates's head, but the superintendent knocked the weapon away as the man fled and the guards' guns blasted away.

Another escapee scuffled with Gates and stabbed the superintendent in the neck. Using Gates as a shield, the prisoner continued to plunge his knife into Gates as he maneuvered out the gate.

As the struggle between Gates and the prisoner continued, inmate Barney Riggs grabbed a weapon dropped by one of the escapees and fired at the prisoner holding the superintendent. The escapee stumbled, and a bullet from one of the guards finally brought him down.

Riggs and another inmate named Sprague attended to the wounded superintendent. Gates later reported:

> I staggered and Riggs caught me by the arm, while another convict named Sprague, placing his hand over my wound to prevent the breath from escaping, assisted me to my room; in addition to this injury, I was badly bruised from the handles of the knives with which the convicts struck me, while I was struggling with them.

The entire episode lasted just a few minutes. All the escapees lay dead or wounded—none escaped. Superintendent Gates never fully recovered from the ordeal and eventually resigned from his position. After many years of severe pain from the injuries he sustained in the breakout, he committed suicide in 1896.

Local Quechen Indians, who were excellent trackers, hunted down fleeing prisoners who made it out the sally port and tasted freedom for a short while. Each convict returned to the prison, dead or alive, brought a reward of fifty dollars.

When the first female convict arrived at the prison gate, trouble and contention came with her.

Lizzie Gallagher, convicted of manslaughter, arrived at Yuma Prison in November 1878. With no separate facility for women prisoners at the time and prison officials finding no way to keep her from the rest of the convicts, she was immediately transferred to the Yuma City Jail for "safekeeping." She returned to the prison in October 1879 and received a pardon about a month later, much to the relief of prison officials.

Women's quarters were eventually dug out of a rocky incline, but as reported to the Board of Control in 1897, this section of the prison was no more than a rat hole, "a den of horror and no remedy for this state of affairs exists without a large expenditure of money under the present conditions."

Many women received early pardons just to relieve them of living under appalling, unsanitary conditions.

Although the prison suffered from overcrowding during its entire tenure, continued improvements kept the place tolerable. Former riverboat captain Ingalls, who served two terms as superintendent, added additional cells and provided space for carpenter, shoe, and tailor shops along with a blacksmith barn. After excavating one of the surroundings hills, he doubled the size of the prison yard and built the west and north granite walls, which stood approximately sixteen to eighteen feet high with a roughly eight-foot base tapering to five feet at the top. This provided enough foot room for guards to patrol the perimeter. Ingalls also oversaw construction of the superintendent's house and five guard stations.

In 1885 Ingalls brought electricity into the prison, a luxury even the city of Yuma did not enjoy for another ten years.

Medical aid for the prisoners was almost nonexistent, except for occasional visits from local doctors. According to an 1891 report to the territorial governor, the sick were detained in one of the corridors running through the main cellblock.

By 1892 a tunnel dug out of the hillside sufficed as a hospital. Madora Ingalls might be considered the angel of the prisoners, as she continually tried to improve their lot by insisting on better health care and cleanliness throughout the prison.

When a new adobe hospital was built above the main cellblock in 1902, "an abundance of light and ventilation" washed across rooms that offered hot running water and bathrooms. Now with two wards (one to isolate tuberculosis patients), a screened-in porch surrounding three sides of the infirmary, and an ample supply of drugs and surgical instruments, one of the attending physicians reported, "The sanitary condition maintained in the hospital is not excelled by that in any similar institution of my acquaintance."

At its peak, over four hundred prisoners resided within the prison. Although each cell was built for two men, smaller cells now contained four to six men while larger ones held up to a dozen inmates. Construction continued throughout the prison's history, but eventually, even the addition of new cells could not contain the growing convict population.

In September 1909, a new prison was completed in Florence, Arizona, and the last remaining convicts at Yuma moved to the new facility. Title to the prison reverted to the city of Yuma, and the facility might have remained abandoned and unused. Circumstances, however, paved the way for a new breed of inmates at the timeworn penitentiary.

Just a year after the last prisoner departed, Yuma High School burned to the ground. With no other facility available, school officials looked to the old penal institution as a temporary school. Parents protested, but with no other place to hold classes, Yuma High School students matriculated at the prison for the next four years. Taking it all in stride, the students called their athletic teams the Yuma Criminals, and those in the honor society were known as "wardens." The term "Crims" is still used today to designate teams from the school.

In 1914 the county hospital utilized the old superintendent's house until it was torn down in 1923 to make way for expansion of the Southern Pacific Railroad. The Veterans of

Foreign Wars occupied the original guards' quarters from 1931 until it burned down in 1960.

During the depression years, transients sought shelter in the tunneled-out cells, and entire homeless families lived inside cubicles formerly occupied by murderers and thieves until they moved on in search of employment. Much of the graffiti inside the cells today dates back to those desperate times.

Civil Defense personnel took over the main guard tower during World War II and used it as an observation site.

Moviemakers found the grounds tempting for western films during the 1930s and 1940s with actors such as John Wayne and Gene Autry moseying around the ancient pokey. The prison still draws in Hollywood and television filmmakers, who continue to film inside and outside the ancient jailed walls.

When curiosity about the penitentiary escalated in 1940, the Works Progress Administration (WPA) built a museum on the grounds of the old prison. The facility was established as an Arizona State Historic Park on January 1, 1961.

Work continues on Yuma Prison. Crumbling wall sections, the main cellblock area, and the exercise yards need to be restored.

The well-worn graveyard contains the remains of 104 inmates who died during the years when the prison was filled with desperadoes. Many succumbed to tuberculosis, a few were bitten by rattlesnakes, several were murdered by other inmates, a handful committed suicide, others died in accidents, and then there are those who were felled while trying to escape.

Most of the graves have been destroyed by time and vandalism, but the cemetery remains as a reminder that the hilltop hacienda served as a commanding deterrent for those early outlaws who walked on the wrong side of the law.

Bibliography

Barnes, Will C. *Arizona Place Names*. Tucson: University of
  Arizona Press, 1988.
Erwin, Allen A. *The Southwest of John H. Slaughter, 1841–1922*.
  Spokane, Wash.: The Arthur H. Clark Company, 1965.
Genung, Dan B. *Death in His Saddlebags: Charles Baldwin Genung,
  Arizona Pioneer*. Manhattan, Kans.: Sunflower University Press,
  1992.
Prassel, Frank Richard. *The Great American Outlaw: A Legacy of
  Fact and Fiction*. Norman, Okla.: University of Oklahoma
  Press, 1993.
Rasch, Philip J. *Desperadoes of Arizona Territory*. Laramie, Wyo.:
  National Association for Outlaw and Lawman History, Inc. In
  affiliation with the University of Wyoming, 1999.
Sheridan, Thomas E. *Arizona: A History*. Tucson: University of
  Arizona Press, 1995.
Sonnichsen, C. L. *Billy King's Tombstone: The Private Life of an
  Arizona Boom Town*. Tucson: University of Arizona Press,
  1972.
Wagoner, Jay J. *Arizona Territory 1863–1912: A Political History*.
  Tucson: University of Arizona Press, 1970.

The Wickenburg Massacre

Barney, James M. "The Wickenburg Massacre." *The Sheriff* 5 no. 3
  (October 1946): 15–22.
Farish, Thomas Edwin. *History of Arizona*. Phoenix: State of
  Arizona, 1918.
Hawkins, Helen B. *A History of Wickenburg to 1875*. Wickenburg:
  Maricopa County Historical Society, 1971. Thesis, Arizona
  State College, 1950.

Miller, Joseph, ed. *The Arizona Story*. New York: Hastings House, 1952.

Smith, Bill W., comp. *A Collection of Newspaper Articles, Letters, and Reports Regarding the Wickenburg Massacre and Subsequent Camp Date Creek Incident*. Phoenix: Bill W. Smith, 1989.

Truman, Ben C. *Occidental Sketches*. San Francisco: San Francisco News Company, 1881.

Wilson, R. Michael. *Drenched in Blood, Rigid in Death: The True Story of the Wickenburg Massacre*. Las Vegas: Juniper Twig Books, 2000.

Frank Nashville "Buckskin Frank" Leslie

Bailey, Lynn R., and Don Chaput. *Cochise County Stalwarts: A Who's Who of the Territorial Years*. Vols. 1 and 2. Tucson: Westernlore Press, 2000.

Breakenridge, William M. *Helldorado: Bringing the Law to the Mesquite*. Lincoln, Nebr.: University of Nebraska Press, 1992. Originally published 1928.

Chafin, Carl, ed. *The Private Journals of George Whitwell Parsons*. Vol. 2. Tombstone, AZ: Cochise Classics, 1997.

Chaput, Don. *"Buckskin Frank" Leslie*. Tucson: Westernlore Press, 1999.

Martin, Douglas D. *Silver, Sex and Six Guns: Tombstone Saga of the Life of Buckskin Frank Leslie*. Tombstone, AZ: Tombstone Epitaph, 1962.

Rickards, Colin. *"Buckskin Frank" Leslie: Gunman of Tombstone*. El Paso, Texas: Texas Western College Press, 1964.

Traywick, Ben T. *The Chronicles of Tombstone*. Tombstone, AZ: Red Marie's Bookstore, 1986.

The Grime/Hawley Heist

Bigando, Robert. *Globe, Arizona: The Life and Times of a Western Mining Town, 1864–1917*. Globe, AZ: American Globe Publishing Company, 1989.

Hayes, Jess G. *Boots and Bullets: The Life and Times of John W. Wentworth*. Tucson: University of Arizona Press, 1967.

Heiter, Paul T. "Popular Justice Run Amok: The Globe Lynchings of 1882." Yuma, AZ: Paper presented at Arizona Historical Society Convention, 1999.

Walters, Lorenzo D. *Tombstone's Yesterday* manuscript collection, 1928–1928. Tucson: Arizona Historical Society.

———. *Tombstone's Yesterday*. Glorieta, N. Mex.: The Rio Grande Press, Inc., 1968. First published 1928.

Wilson, R. Michael. *Crime & Punishment in Early Arizona*. Las Vegas: Stagecoach Books, 2004.

Woody, Clara T., and Milton L. Schwartz. *Globe, Arizona*. Tucson: The Arizona Historical Society, 1977.

John Peters Ringo

"Almost a Tragedy." *Tucson Weekly Citizen*. January 22, 1882.

"A Social Game." *Tombstone Daily Nugget*. August 11, 1881. Reprinted from "A Game of Draw." *Arizona Weekly Star*. August 11, 1881.

Breakenridge, William M. *Helldorado: Bringing the Law to the Mesquite*. Lincoln, Nebr.: University of Nebraska Press, 1992. First published 1928.

Burns, Walter Noble. *Tombstone: An Iliad of the Southwest*. Albuquerque: University of New Mexico Press, 1999. First published 1927.

Burrows, Jack. *John Ringo: The Gunfighter Who Never Was*. Tucson: University of Arizona Press, 1987.

"Death of John Ringo. His Body Found in Morse's Canyon – Probably Suicide." *Tombstone Daily Epitaph*. July 19, 1882.

Franklin, A. M. "John Ringo." Franklin Family manuscript file.
Arizona Historical Society, MS 0270.

Gatto, Steve. "Johnny Ringo: Land and Cattle Speculator?"
Quarterly of the National Association for Outlaw and Lawman
History, Inc. October-December 1994: 9-10.

———. *Johnny Ringo*. Lansing, Mich.: Protar House, 2002.

———. *John Ringo: The Reputation of a Deadly Gunman*. Tucson,
AZ: San Simon Publishing Co., 1995.

"His Last Shot. The King of the Cowboys Sends a Bullet Through
His Brain." *Arizona Daily Star*. July 18, 1882.

John Ringo Family History. Accessed at www.clantongang.com/
oldwest/ganringo.html, on October 29, 2010.

Johnson, David. *John Ringo*. Stillwater, Okla.: Barbed Wire Press,
1996.

Thomas, Bob. "Was Wyatt Earp Ringo's Killer?" *Arizona Daily
Star*. January 26, 1964.

"Tombstone Topics." *Tucson Weekly Citizen*. January 29, 1882.

Traywick, Ben T. *John Peters Ringo: Mythical Gunfighter*.
Tombstone, AZ: Red Marie's Bookstore, 1987.

James Addison Reavis

Burgess, Glenn, ed. *Mount Graham Profiles: Volume 2, Ryder
Ridgeway Collection*. Safford, AZ: Graham County Historical
Society, 1988.

Cookridge, E. H. *The Baron of Arizona*. New York: Ballantine
Books, 1967.

Farrell, Robert J., ed. *They Left Their Mark*. Phoenix: Arizona
Department of Transportation, 1997.

Powell, Donald M. "The 'Baron of Arizona' Self Revealed: A Letter
to His Lawyer in 1894." *Arizona and the West 1*, no. 2 (summer
1959): 161–73.

———. *The Peralta Grant: James Addison Reavis and the Barony of*

Arizona. Norman, Okla.: University of Oklahoma Press, 1960.

Tipton, Will M. "The Prince of Imposters." *Land of Sunshine* 8, nos. 3 & 4 (February and March 1898): 106–18, 161–70.

Charles P. Stanton

Barkdull, Tom. *Lonesome Walls: An Odyssey Through Ghost Towns of the Old West*. New York: Exposition Press, 1971.

Crombie, M. Katherine, Chris T. Gholson, Dante S. Lauretta, and Erik B. Melchiorre. *Rich Hill: The History of Arizona's Most Amazing Gold District*. Tucson, AZ: Golden Retriever Publications, 2002.

Esenwein, William. *The Private Empire of Charlie P. Stanton, King of Con Men*. Stanton, AZ: Esenwein, 1973.

Genung, Charles Baldwin, comp. *Yavapai Country Memories, 1863–1894*, nos. 43 & 44 (spring and fall 1982): 66–69.

Gould, P. B. *The Irish Lord: Charles B. Stanton*. Congress, AZ: PBG Press, 2005.

Lauer, Charles D. *Tales of Arizona Territory*. Phoenix: Golden West Publishers, 1990.

Stano, Mary G. "Charles Stanton: He Ruled a Town by Betrayal and Murder." *The Nevadan Today*. March 26, 1989.

The Apache Kid

Forrest, Earle R., and Edwin B. Hill. *Lone War Trail of Apache Kid*. Pasadena, Calif.: Trail's End Publishing Co., Inc., 1947.

Freeman, Dr. M. P. *The Dread Apache: That Early-Day Scourge of the Southwest*. Tucson, AZ: n.p., 1915.

de la Garza, Phyllis. *The Apache Kid*. Tucson, AZ: Westernlore Press, 1995.

Genung, Dan B. Genung Reminscences manuscript collection. Tucson: Arizona Historical Society.

Genung Jr., Dan B. "The Death of the Apache Kid." *Arizona*

Highways Magazine. November 1995: 32–35.

Pool, Frank M. "The Apache Kid." *The Sheriff* 6, no. 2 (March 1947): 18–24.

Ringgold, Jennie Parks. *Frontier Days in the Southwest: Pioneer Days in Old Arizona*. San Antonio, Texas: The Naylor Company, 1952.

Robinson, Sherry. *Apache Voices: Their Stories of Survival As Told to Eve Ball*. Albuquerque: University of New Mexico Press, 2000.

Sparks, William. *The Apache Kid, a Bear Fight and Other True Stories of the Old West*. Los Angeles: Skelton Publishing Company, 1926.

Wharfield, H. B. "Footnotes to History: Apache Kid and the Record." *The Journal of Arizona History* 6, no. 1 (spring 1965): 37–46.

Williamson, Dan R. "The Apache Kid: Renegade of the West." *Arizona Highways Magazine* 15, no. 5 (May 1939): 14–17.

Wham Paymaster Robbery

Ball, Larry D. *Ambush at Bloody Run: The Wham Paymaster Robbery of 1889*. Tucson: The Arizona Historical Society, 2000.

————. *The United States Marshals of New Mexico and Arizona Territories, 1846–1912*. Albuquerque: University of New Mexico Press, 1978.

Block, Eugene B. *Great Stagecoach Robbers of the West*. New York: Doubleday & Company, Inc., 1962.

Marshall, Otto Miller. *The Wham Paymaster Robbery, Boldest in Arizona History, May 11, 1889*. Sponsored and distributed by the Pima Chamber of Commerce, April 1967.

Schubert, Frank N. *Black Valor: Buffalo Soldiers and the Medal of Honor, 1870–1898*. Wilmington, Del.: Scholarly Resources, Inc., 1997.

————. *Voices of the Buffalo Soldier: Records, Reports, and*

Recollections of Military Life and Service in the West.
Albuquerque: University of New Mexico Press, 2003.
Upton, Larry T., and Larry D. Ball. "Who Robbed Major
Wham? Facts and Folklore Behind Arizona's Great Paymaster
Robbery." *Journal of Arizona History* 38, no. 2 (summer 1997):
99–134.

Augustine Chacón

Edwards, Harold L. "This is the Greatest Day of My Life: The
Hanging of Augustin Chacón." *True West.* November 1995:
14–21.
Burgess, Glenn, ed. *Mount Graham Profiles, Volume 2, Ryder
Ridgeway Collection.* Safford, AZ: Graham County Historical
Society, 1988.
Rickards, Colin. "The Hairy One—Arizona's Deadly Bandit." *The
West: True Stories of the Old West* 14, no. 1 (December 1970):
30–31, 56–64.

James Fleming Parker

Allen, Paul L., and Peter M. Pegnam. *Arizona Territory: Baptism in
Blood.* Tucson: Tucson Citizen Publishing Company, 1990.
Miller, Joseph, ed. *The Arizona Story.* New York: Hastings House,
1952.
Trimble, Marshall. *Arizona: A Cavalcade of History.* Tucson:
Treasure Chest Publications, 1989.
———. *Arizona Highways: The Law of the Gun.* Phoenix: Arizona
Department of Transportation, State of Arizona, 1997.
Way, Thomas E. *The Parker Story.* Prescott, AZ: Prescott Graphics,
1981.
Weiner, Melissa Ruffner. *Prescott Yesteryears: Life in Arizona's First
Territorial Capital.* Prescott, AZ: Primrose Press, 1979.

Wilson, R. Michael. *Crime & Punishment in Early Arizona*. Las Vegas: Stagecoach Books, 2004.

Pearl Hart

Aikman, Duncan. *Calamity Jane and the Lady Wildcats*. New York: Henry Holt and Company, 1927.

Allen, Paul L., and Peter M. Pegnam. *Arizona Territory: Baptism in Blood*. Tucson: Tucson Citizen Publishing Company, 1990.

Armitage, Shelley. "Pearl Hart: Desperate Woman or Desperado?" *With Badges and Bullets: Lawmen & Outlaws in the Old West*. Richard W. Etulain & Glenda Riley, eds. Golden, Colo.: Fulcrum Publishing, 1999.

Brent, William, and Milarde Brent. *The Hell Hole*. Yuma, AZ: William Brent and Milarde Brent, 1962.

Brown, Wynne. *More than Petticoats: Remarkable Arizona Women*. Guilford, Conn.: Globe Pequot Press, 2003.

Hart, Pearl. "An Arizona Episode." *Cosmopolitan* 27, no. 6 (October 1899): 673–77.

Horan, James D. *Desperate Women*. New York: G. P. Putnam's Sons, 1952.

Klungness, Elizabeth J. *Prisoners in Petticoats: The Yuma Territorial Prison and Its Women*. Yuma, AZ: Yuma County Historical Society Publications, 1993.

Walters, Lorenzo D. *Tombstone's Yesterday* manuscript collection, 1928-1928. Tucson: Arizona Historical Society.

———. *Tombstone's Yesterday*. Glorieta, N. Mex.: The Rio Grande Press, Inc., 1968. First published 1928.

Wilson, R. Michael. *Encyclopedia of Stagecoach Robbery in Arizona*. Las Vegas: RaMA Press, 2003.

Woody, Clara T., and Milton L. Schwartz. *Globe, Arizona*. Tucson: The Arizona Historical Society, 1977.

Albert Wright "Burt" Alvord

Block, Eugene B. *Great Train Robberies of the West*. New York: Coward-McCann, Inc., 1959.

Bond, Ervin. *Percy Bowden: Born to be a Frontier Lawman*. Douglas, AZ: Bond, 1976.

Chaput, Don. *The Odyssey of Burt Alvord: Lawman, Train Robber, Fugitive*. Tucson, AZ: Westernlore Press, 2000.

Coolidge, Dane. *Fighting Men of the West*. New York: E. P. Dutton & Co., Inc., 1932.

Haley, J. Evetts. *Jeff Milton: A Good Man with a Gun*. Norman, Okla.: University of Oklahoma Press, 1948.

Hendricks, George D. *The Bad Man of the West*. San Antonio, Texas: The Naylor Company, 1942.

Patterson, Richard. *The Train Robbery Era: An Encyclopedic History*. Boulder, Colo.: Pruett Publishing Company, 1991.

Ringgold, Jennie Parks. *Frontier Days in the Southwest*. San Antonio, Texas: The Naylor Company, 1952.

Theobald, John and Lillian. *Wells Fargo in Arizona Territory*. Tempe: Arizona Historical Foundation, 1978.

White, Scott, as told to John Edwin Hogg. "Bad Men's Nemesis: The adventures and experiences of an Arizona sheriff, in a land and a time when a man often wore a moustache, but always wore a gun." *Touring Topics*, April 1931: 25–26.

Cecil Creswell

Brisendine, J. E. "The Cecil Creswell Story." Winslow, AZ: Old Trails Museum, 1954.

Cameron, Bill. "Suicide of 'Cecil' Ends One of Strangest Stories in Colorful History of the County." *Winslow Mail*, March 12, 1954: 1,5.

Lowe, Sam. *Mysteries and Legends of Arizona: True Stories of the Unsolved and Unexplained*. Guilford, Conn.: Globe Pequot Press, 2010.

Sheridan, Thomas E. *Arizona: A History*. Tucson: University of
    Arizona Press, 1995.
Thomas, Bob. "Cecil Creswell: The Astonishing Double Life of
    Frontier Rancher." *Arizona Highways*. October 1995: 18-23.

Yuma Territorial Prison

Anable, Michael E., and Kenneth E. Travous. *The Prison Chronicle:
    Yuma Territorial Prison's Colorful Past*. Phoenix: Arizona State
    Parks Board, 1999.
Hayhurst, Hal M. "Yuma's Territorial Prison." *Arizona Highways*.
    May 1944: 32-35, 41.
Hubbard, Paul G. "Life in the Arizona Territorial Prison, 1876-
    1910." *Arizona and the West* 1, no. 4: 317-330.
Jeffrey, John Mason. *Adobe and Iron: the Story of the Arizona
    Territorial Prison at Yuma*. La Jolla, Calif.: Prospect Avenue
    Press, 1969.
———. "Discipline in the Arizona Territorial Prison: Draconian
    Severity or Enlightened Administration?" *Journal of Arizona
    History*. 140-154.
Parker, Lowell. "Prison on the Bluff: Was it Hell Hole or Country
    Club?" Part 2 of 3. Publication unknown. Accessed at Pinal
    County Historical Society, Florence, Arizona.
"The Territorial Prison." *Arizona Republican* 1, no. 98.
Trafzer, Clifford E. *Prison Centennial, 1876-176: A Pictorial History
    of the Arizona Territorial Prison at Yuma*. Yuma, AZ: Rio
    Colorado Press, 1976.
Woznicki, Robert. *The History of Yuma and the Territorial Prison*.
    Tempe, AZ: Robert Woznicki, 1995. Original edition published
    by author in 1968.
"Yuma Penitentiary's Fascinating History is Retold by Pioneer."
    Arizona Republic. April 13, 1938.
"Yuma Prison, Colorful Part of Past." *Florence Reminder and Blade-
    Tribune*, September 27, 1973.

Index

Index

Index

Index

Index

Index

About the Author

Award-winning author, historian, and lecturer Jan Cleere writes extensively about the desert Southwest, particularly the people who first settled this untamed territory. Her work reflects her love of the west and her knowledge of western history. Her articles have appeared in regional and national publications.

She is the author of two other Globe Pequot Press titles, *More Than Petticoats: Remarkable Nevada Women* and *Amazing Girls of Arizona: True Stories of Young Pioneers*. She resides in Tucson, Arizona, under the shadow of the Catalina Mountains with her husband and the myriad wildlife that visits her desert home.